EXPERIENTIAL
ASTROLOGY

Some Other Titles from Falcon Press

Antero Alli
- *Angel Tech: A Modern Shaman's Guide to Reality Selection*
- *The Eight-Circuit Brain*
- *State of Emergence*
- *The Akashic Record Player*

Christopher S. Hyatt, Ph.D. & Antero Alli
- *A Modern Shaman's Guide to a Pregnant Universe*

Christopher S. Hyatt, Ph.D. & Calvin Iwema
- *Energized Hypnosis (book, videos & audios)*

Christopher S. Hyatt, Ph.D.
- *Undoing Yourself with Energized Meditation and Other Devices*
- *To Lie Is Human: Not Getting Caught Is Divine*
- *Secrets of Western Tantra: The Sexuality of the Middle Path*

Christopher S. Hyatt, Ph.D. with contributions by Wm. S. Burroughs, Timothy Leary, Robert Anton Wilson et al.
- *Rebels & Devils: The Psychology of Liberation*

Peter J. Carroll
- *The Chaos Magick Audios*
- *PsyberMagick*

Phil Hine
- *Condensed Chaos: An Introduction to Chaos Magic*
- *Prime Chaos: Adventures in Chaos Magic*
- *The Pseudonomicon*

Israel Regardie
- *The Complete Golden Dawn System of Magic*
- *New Wings for Daedalus*
- *The Golden Dawn Audios*

Joseph C. Lisiewski, Ph.D.
- *Ceremonial Magic and the Power of Evocation*
- *Kabbalistic Handbook for the Practicing Magician*

Steven Heller
- *Monsters & Magical Sticks: There's No Such Thing as Hypnosis?*

For up-to-the-minute information on prices and availability, please visit our website at http://originalfalcon.com

~ XA ~
EXPERIENTIAL ASTROLOGY

From the Map To the Territory

by
Antero Alli

Preface by
Rick Merlin Levine

THE *Original* FALCON PRESS
TEMPE, ARIZONA, U.S.A.

Copyright © 2021 C.E. by Antero Alli

All rights reserved. No part of this book, in part or in whole, may be reproduced, transmitted, or utilized, in any form or by any means, electronic or mechanical, including photocopying, recording, or by any information storage and retrieval system, without permission in writing from the publisher, except for brief quotations in critical articles, books and reviews.

International Standard Book Number: 978-1-61869-715-8
ISBN: 978-1-61869-716-5 (mobi)
ISBN: 978-1-61869-717-2 (ePub)
Library of Congress Control Number: 9781618697158

First Edition 2022
First eBook Edition 2022
Second Edition 2022

Cover by James Koehnline

Address all inquiries to:
The Original Falcon Press
1753 East Broadway Road #101-277
Tempe, AZ 85282 U.S.A.
(or)
PO Box 3540
Silver Springs NV 89429 U.S.A.
website: http://www.originalfalcon.com
email: info@originalfalcon.com

Ah, not to be cut off, not through the slightest partition shut out from the law of the stars. The inner—what is it? if not intensified sky, hurled through with birds and deep with the winds of homecoming.

— Rainer Maria Rilke

Table of Contents

ACKNOWLEDGEMENTS 9

PREFACE
by Rick Merlin Levine 11

INTRODUCTION
How This Book Works
  The Embodiment Bias of Experiential Astrology 16
Five Misconceptions About Astrology
  Exposing Clichés and Busting Stereotypes 21

THE 12 SYMBOLIC SETS
Astrology as a Language of Associations
  Forces, States and Styles: The Planets, Houses and Signs Revisioned 26
  Aries, Mars, 1st House (State of Being), and the Ascendant .. 34
  Taurus, Venus, 2nd House (State of Survival) 39
  Gemini, Mercury, 3rd House (State of Mind) 44
  Cancer, the Moon, 4th House (Sustaining State), and the Nadir 48
  Leo, the Sun, 5th House (Creative State) 54
  Virgo, Mercury, 6th House (State of Employment) 60
  Libra, Venus, 7th House (State of Intimacy), the Descendent . 65
  Scorpio, Pluto, Mars, 8th House (State of Surrender) 70
  Sagittarius, Jupiter, 9th House (State of Faith) 79
  Capricorn, Saturn, 10th House (Professional State), the Midheaven 85
  Aquarius, Uranus, 11th House (Community State) 92
  Pisces, Neptune, 12th House (State of the Soul) 97

ESSENTIAL RESEARCH TASKS
Experimenting with States, Forces & Styles 105

HOROSCOPE EXAMPLES
Excerpts from Three Natal Readings...........107

THEORY AND PRAXIS
The Nodal Axis, Asteroids, Chiron & Major Aspects
- *The Nodal Axis* 116
- *The Four Major Asteroids* 126
- *Comet Chiron & Punk Rock* 135
- *The Six Major Aspects* 139

INTERPRETIVE TECHNIQUES
For the Investigative Astrologer
- *Intercepted Houses and Empty Houses* 156
- *Mercury Logosis and The Venusian Dilemma* 159
- *Guiding Planet and the Dispositor Planet to North Node* ... 162
- *Grand Trines and Grand Crosses* 165
- *T-Squares and Yods* 169

TRANSITS
Rites of Passage
- *Tracking the Timing of Change* 174
- *Transpersonal Transits* 183

PLANETARY FORCES AS SEXUAL REALITIES
The Complex Playing Fields of Sexuality
- *Part One: Sun, Moon, Mercury, Venus, Mars* 196
- *Part Two: Jupiter, Saturn, Chiron, Uranus, Neptune and Pluto* 206
- *Part Three: A Planetary Ménage à Trois Wherein the Author Submits to the Earth* 218

AFTERWORD 223

ABOUT THE AUTHOR 229

ACKNOWLEDGEMENTS

The first individuals I count as mentors, Michael Symonds and David Rosenbloom, two talented clairvoyants whose guidance I followed through related esoteric trainings in Berkeley in the late 1970's. Michael taught the psychic art of seeing and interpreting the human aura, a practice I continued until 1987. These auric talents eventually transformed into the intuitive foundation of my astrological practice. David initiated me into a non-performance physical theatre as a way to access energy sources in the body *as movement resources.* His early "paratheatrical" experiments inspired forty years of ongoing development into the somatic discipline of Paratheatre inspiring the *embodied bias* behind this book and most everything else I do.

In the early 1980's, I studied with astrologer Helen Jaspers during my brief residence in the Carmel area on the central California coast. Helen introduced me to the idea that astrology is, first and foremost, *a language,* which became a central principle in my astrological practice.

In the mid-1980's in Boulder Colorado, I met astrologer Robert Buchanan and was impressed by his sharp wit, sly wisdom, and sense of humor. He had a way of quickly and accurately pinpointing the inner workings of any chart by framing everything he saw within a story. As Robert would say, *"Everybody has a story; it's in the chart."*

Many thanks to creative artist Bat St. Chip for their original line drawings of the twelve zodiac signs as the chapter headings for the "12 SYMBOLIC SETS" section, the "Moon Tree" image, and the "Judgement" image in the "Afterword".

The boldly libertine artworks near the end of the book ("Planetary Forces as Sexual Realities" Parts 2 & 3) were created by the Australian pantheist artist/filmmaker and ritualist Orryelle Defenestrate, who I've had the pleasure of meeting over the years.

The book cover art is by my wayback friend, collage genius James Koehnline.

I am grateful for Rob Brezsny's poetic interpretations of his astrological omens in his weekly "Free Will" astrology column and elsewhere. Rob's consistent insurrection of the Poetic Imagination continues to inspire me and his many readers.

I am thankful for the wonderful story-telling narrative style of astrological bard Steven Forrest whose books guided my early studies of the celestial language.

Last but never least, I am deeply grateful for Sylvi, my multi-talented wife of twenty-six years and counting. With assistance from our good friend Robin Coomer, Sylvi was the chief proofreader of this book, correcting my poor grammar while kindly chiding me for my flagrant abuse of the comma. Now that the book is done, I look forward to playing more music and making another movie with you.

In gratitude,
Antero

PREFACE
by Rick Merlin Levine

I was thrilled when Antero Alli asked me if I would write a Preface for his new astrology book. I am even more thrilled now that I have read it, and have had a chance to think about it. Confession: this is not the first book by Antero that I've read, so I knew that I would have to set my expectations aside because everything that he writes is not what one expects. I remember reading *Astrologik: The Interpretive Art of Astrology* back in 1990 (was that *really* over thirty years ago?!) and being both excited and bothered by the book. I was excited because it was such a fresh approach to a subject I was already quite familiar with. I was bothered by it because it challenged some of my astrological assumptions and I couldn't just walk away from his ideas, however revolutionary they were. I was bothered by his eclectic approach, which was a good thing because it changed the way I think about this amazing branch of knowledge called astrology that Antero and I share.

But, of course, astrology is not ours. It belongs to humanity. We, Antero and I (and key figures throughout history, plus an ever-growing population of aficionados, students, and professionals), study astrology because it touches our souls. We are intrigued by how the cosmos can, in its immensity, create meaning in the transient lives of those humans who choose to step outside the boundaries of consensus reality to explore this ancient wisdom that holds the special position of being damned by both science and religion. I have always taken pride in the fact that as an astrologer, I escaped from the confines of fear-based religion and broke free of the constraints imposed by the traditional academic view of reality. I viewed myself as sort of an intellectual outlaw, seeking to live by a higher code than the restraining laws of the land. That is, until I met a real outlaw in the form of Antero Alli. Antero didn't only rebel against the intellectual *status quo*; he took it farther by stepping outside the trappings of astrology, itself.

I was bothered by Antero's eagerness to re-language some of astrology's most basic concepts. Planets were, in *Astrologik*, no longer planets; they became "forces." The houses became "states" and the zodiacal signs became "styles." In *Experiential Astrology*, Antero writes, "My job as 'astrologer' is all about *languaging my perceptions.*" His insightful use of language has, in this new book, added to forces, states and styles. One of the basic techniques in the astrologer's toolbox is the "house ruler," the sign that labels the cusp (or cutting edge) of each of the twelve houses. Antero refers to these house rulers as "governors." It's another re-languaging concept that works.

As a practicing astrologer, I have been deeply involved in a branch of contemporary astrology called, "experiential astrology," so I was eager to read about Antero's perspective on this work. True to form, that is not what I got. This is absolutely a book about experiential astrology, but not the experiential astrology that is being practiced by others. Again, Antero is using language to change how we think. In my world, experiential astrology consisted of a range of techniques like "astrodrama" (where students would act out the planetary energies), or "planet walks" (where they would practice physical walking rhythms to conjure the various archetypes). I have been attracted to experiential astrology because it gets students and clients out of their heads and into their bodies. But it is specifically technique oriented.

Antero Alli's *Experiential Astrology* is right up the same alley. But it revisions all of astrology as experientially based, rather than being relegated to a detached intellectual exercise. Ultimately, this book lays the groundwork to understand how all astrology is experiential. In his words, "Experiential Astrology encourages firsthand experience of the living forces symbolized in the horoscope. As such, this approach can be loosely defined as animistic and shamanic." Yes and yes! Give me more of this, please.

Experiential Astrology

Experiential Astrology (XA) is not a book of answers or an astrological cookbook. Nor does it need to be, since there is no shortage of books that tell us, "Planet A in such-and-such a sign and house means blah blah blah." *XA* is not a roadmap to chart interpretation. It is not a linear "how to" book that says start here and follow these steps to reach your destination. *XA* is a smorgasbord. It is a multi-dimensional mosaic that lays out an alternative way of seeing the variety of astrological experience. It's not quite a beginner's book, but neither does it require knowledge of advanced techniques. In fact, a minimal understanding of the planets, signs, houses and aspects might be all that is required to gain the unique perspective this book offers. On the other end of the spectrum, advanced students or even practicing professionals could stand to have their view of astrology shaken up a bit. I've been studying astrology for over 50 years (yikes!) and Antero has served me up a rich meal with much food for thought. It will take some time for me to digest all the tidbits that he has brought to my table.

I particularly loved Antero's section on misconceptions about astrology, because he clearly states things most astrologers think about. But sometimes his conclusions are askew of the traditional astrological party line, and it's refreshing to consider his ideas about astrology horoscope columns, fortune-telling, fate and destiny, and more.

In the part about the zodiac itself, Antero leads us on a nontraditional romp through the elements and modalities, the signs (styles) and houses (states), their relationship to the planets (forces), and the role of the house cusps (governors). We learn about the polarity (balance point) of each house and the shadow each planet casts. We learn about the Ascendant, major asteroids, Chiron and the Lunar Nodes. We are given a cook's tour of planetary dispositors, planetary configurations, and the significance of timing (transits). But, as stated before, this is not a detached and analytical approach. It is a personal disclosure. It is about the embodiment of the astrological archetypes. It's a story about how the symbols come alive, about how we can use the astrological language to make the invisible visible, the subconscious conscious.

As a significant part of embodiment, we are led through a unique and revealing section about each of the planets as sexual realities. Although many astrologers have written about astrology and sexuality, Antero creates a template that is quite ingenious and filled with solid and useful observations.

Although we are given excerpts from a few of Antero's readings, they are not just examples of how it all comes together. They are food for thought to prime the pump for the research exercises throughout the book. Again and again, Antero brings his thoughts back to the reader. How does this work in *your* chart? What happened in *your* life when this or that transit occurred?

I love Antero's writing because he is a true innovator. I think of myself as less centrist and traditional than many astrologers, yet Antero reminds me how wide our perspective can be and how vast the cosmos is. But Antero is also an artist of language, a poet. Throughout the book, he casually drops bombs that combine powerful depth of perception with the creative magic of poetry. For example, writing about Neptune and "The Illusion of Reality," he says, "Neptune transits require the sonar of intuition and the somatic compass of our five senses." I'll quote him again on that!

Astrology eludes classification. It's not a science, nor is it a pseudoscience. It's more than a science. Astrology is an art form, but it's not just art. It is the embodiment of the magic of sacred geometry. One can read a few books and, to some degree, mechanically ply the craft of astrology. It has been said that astronomy is a glove, and astrology is the living hand inside the glove. Modern science is ultimately distracted by the glove, even to the extent of denying the reality of the conscious metaphysical energy that moves the glove. Technique is assuredly an important part of astrology. But it is the embodiment, the experience, and the use of language to describe the invisible that makes astrology come alive. Antero has given us an offering intended for the gods and goddesses. It is up to each of us to take this offering, to personalize it, and to use it as a tool in our journey into experiential astrology.

— Rick Levine, Redmond, WA

INTRODUCTION

How This Book Works
The Embodiment Bias of Experiential Astrology

Numerous systems of astrology exist throughout the world and almost every culture has its own star-mapping system informed by its history, mythology and cultural bias. Due to so many cultural and religious differences, these astrological systems often disagree and even find fault with each other. The system I have been studying and practicing since 1985 is *Western Tropical Astrology*. As a European born in Finland and raised in eastern Canada and in California, Western Tropical felt like a good fit.

As a 12th house Scorpio Sun conjunct Scorpio Ascendant, I enjoy exposing and exploring the contraries within human nature, not as dualities but as complex expressions of a larger changing totality. I view each astrological sign and planet as having a bright side and a dark side, its brilliance and its shadow. I also assume that all twelve signs exist within each individual as different facets and dimensions of personality at various degrees of expression and latency. We may be more multi-faceted than we think or, more to the point, we may be more multi-faceted than we *can* think.

I don't believe the planets control our fates. I interpret planetary symbols in the horoscope as a colorful language of *living forces* residing within the Body itself and in the world we inhabit. These forces seem *autonomous*—meaning they are not always under conscious control. More often, they find expression through us without our conscious awareness. When these forces can be recognized and accepted, they can be more consciously integrated into our personalities—if that's what we want. These forces are symbolized by the planets, the Sun, and the Moon in the natal horoscope. Using this map to gain access to the vital territory of our actual lives forms the basis of this book and why it's called *Experiential Astrology* (hereafter referred to as *XA*).

Experiential Astrology

This book was written for those with a rudimentary grasp of the Signs, Planets, Houses and Aspects, and an eye for new ways of seeing and thinking. The origins or the ancient history of astrology will not be covered, nor will any arguments be presented for or against its academic legitimacy. Certain ideas here will contradict tradition, such as the notion that some planets are "exalted" or in "detriment" or "in their fall" depending on the sign they're in; or that there's such a thing as a "bad" or "horrible" chart. Nonsense! Here in the 21st century Aquarian age, these archaic ideas appear to me as symptoms of a previous Piscean Age pathological victim-bias. The aim of this book is to offer methods, insights and opportunities to test and determine the value and purpose of astrology for yourself. And, maybe, dismantle the victim archetype within you as you go.

The study and practice of XA requires *critical thinking, intuition and imagination*. Critical thinking can help discern the difference between the map and the territory, the chart, and the actual life it represents. Intuition supports a more *direct experience* of the living forces represented by the planetary symbols. Direct experience means experience minimally mediated by dogma, rigid and overly literal thinking, morality and the compulsive need to be right. When critical thinking and intuition can work together in more meaningful ways, imagination is free to explore more poetic interpretations of astrology. Sometimes an uncanny accuracy follows a more poetic interpretation, something that makes no sense to the analytical mind, yet occurs nevertheless. I3: Intellect, Intuition, Imagination.

Everyone has a bias informing *how they know truth*, whether they're aware of that bias or not. In astrological language there can be at least twelve ways to know truth, symbolized by Jupiter, its house, and sign. For example, my natal 6th house Jupiter in the fixed earth sign of Taurus symbolizes how I know truth *through the senses in somatic, embodied experiences and by its utility and application*. This also expresses the bias behind this book. It's a pragmatic philosophical outlook that may or may not appeal to those biased by more heavily theoretical orientations. As Taurus also symbolizes what we value and find worthwhile, whatever I find worth learning typically becomes integrated, embodied in me, and put to work.

The Paratheatre Influence

I never went to Astrology School. I confess to not always knowing why or how astrology works. Whatever I do know about astrology comes from personal experience with interpreting well over a thousand charts since 1985. I also confess to being on a parallel path of Paratheatre (group ritual work) for over forty years (refer to my book, *State of Emergence,* Falcon Press). Though astrology was never incorporated into Paratheatre, the universal forces symbolized in any horoscope were always present in this group ritual work where we learned to access, experience and express these forces in movement, dance and vocal creations that were often cathartic and transformative. (paratheatrical.com)

Universal forces, such as the powers of Earth, Water, Fire and Air—*substances within the Body itself*—are a mainstay in paratheatrical and astrological work alike. Paratheatre nurtures and expands the faculties of *intuition and imagination* through a series of somatic methods for "making the unconscious conscious" within a physical discipline of self-expression. Through Paratheatre, I came to experience the physical body, with its many invisible, interactive biosystems, as the *embodiment of the so-called Subconscious mind.*

By accessing and expressing the internal landscape of impulses, tensions, emotions, sensations, images and the deeper ancestral and archetypal currents, paratheatrical methods opened up an internal spectrum of humanity—*the beautiful and the grotesque, the brilliance and the ignorance, the love and the fear, the weak and the strong.* XA encourages firsthand experience of the living forces symbolized in the horoscope. As such, this approach can be loosely defined as *animistic* and *shamanic.* Not saying I'm a shaman, though some may think so.

Throughout four decades of ongoing Paratheatre work I eventually came to understand my own chart not just as a map, but as a kind of door to a confluence of forces interacting with each other

Experiential Astrology

and the world beyond. This experience increased my empathy when interpreting the charts of others. I don't just read charts but experience something of the world each chart represents. This exhausting process is also why I can only interpret one chart per day. My job as "astrologer" is all about *languaging my perceptions*. When words fail, as they often do, I examine the client's natal Mercury placement for insight on how they might process information to learn how to "speak their language."

The Price of Knowledge

This is not an Everything You Need to Know About Astrology book nor does its author claim any final authority on the topic. Though some traditional astrological ideas are presented, this book intends to rock that boat and get you, the reader, a bit wet. A few secrets will be shared here that some may regret knowing about. Such is the price of knowledge. Whatever you know, or think you know, gets constantly tested against the greater unknowns of life itself.

As all true knowledge-keepers eventually discover, the more we know, the more we realize how much we don't know. Gaining knowledge can be humbling that way and if it's not, you're still probably eating the menu instead of the meal. This is why critical thinking can be necessary for telling the difference between an idea or belief and the reality and experience it represents; the map is not the territory. In this way, XA can be used to *fine-tune our BS detectors* (BS also stands for Belief System).

If you can point your BS detector at yourself, you may start seeing through the BS of the world, and the BS of other people. However, some things once seen cannot be unseen. As you discover more truth about yourself, the world and others, it's up to you to find ways to live with more truth. Truth can be cruel. Telling the truth without compassion *can feel just like cruelty*. Whether that's the self-torment of not living up to some ego-ideal or torturing others with your big truths posing as "absolutes", there's no need to make any truth more serious; truth is already serious enough by itself.

My process of reading the charts of others follows two-steps: 1) *I say what I see* and 2) *I say what that means to me in the most honest and compassionate ways I know how.* Based on client feedback, my astrological interpretations now register anywhere between a 70–80% accuracy rate. This heady percentage can easily persuade others, as well as myself, that I may be right most of time. Whether that's true or not, I don't like the feeling of being right most of the time. As an artist (of cinema, theatre, music), just the idea of being right most of the time makes me laugh, and then makes me nauseous. In my art life, I have come to know uncertainty as a creative state and need to remain open to unknowns just to stay creative.

Astrology can be crazy-making and the mental health of more obsessive and hyper-analytical astrologers can be at risk. To sustain my mental health, I minimize the self-delusion of "being right most of the time" by thinking of all perceptions *as gambles*. I rely on client feedback to determine the degree any of my interpretations are true or not for them; the customer is always right or, at least, I hope so. I also interpret everything in a chart as *tendencies,* not absolutes. Though some tendencies can appear strident enough to simulate absolutes, I still consider them tendencies. Those looking for absolute answers to Life's Big Questions may be disappointed with this book. For those who can still think for themselves and have the imagination to keep dreaming, this book was written for you.

— Antero Alli
Portland, Oregon
October 15, 2021

Five Misconceptions About Astrology

Exposing Clichés and Busting Stereotypes

Many clichés and stereotypes about Astrology have been perpetrated in newspapers, television, films, books, and academic and scientific circles, creating a smokescreen of misunderstanding and ridicule when it comes to Astrology. Here now are what I see as the top five misconceptions about Astrology:

1) Astrology Columns

Published as entertainment, most astrology columns present the celestial language in cliched, stereotyped ways. By over-emphasizing the Sun sign, millions of people have been led to mistakenly identify with their Sun signs alone, often encouraging prejudices against and for other Sun signs—resulting in a mild hallucination of misplaced identity. All seasoned astrologers know that the Sun sign represents a small but important dimension of the entire personality (more on this later). One exception to this is Rob Brezsny's syndicated column "Free Will Astrology". More poet than astrologer, Brezsny's treatment of astrology stimulates the imagination, encouraging readers to think for themselves.

2) Science and Skeptics

Much to their discredit, many astrologers insist that Astrology is a Science. So, when more scientifically-minded skeptics ask for empirical proof of its validity, a conflict of interests naturally arises. Astrology cannot really be proven scientifically because it's actually more of a language, or an art, than a science. Astrology has been mislabeled as a science by well-meaning, misinformed astrologers seeking academic or scientific validation—or perhaps deep-seated unconscious approval from absent fathers. Many centuries ago, when astrology was married to astronomy, it was accepted as a science. But a lot has happened since Descartes' "Meditations" and the Age of Reason when Astrology was dismissed, along with the Tarot, Kabbalah, and other "occult sciences," as a pseudoscience.

Skepticism is not the problem. The most accurate and seasoned astrologers show a keen skeptical eye and a strong capacity for critical thinking. The problem is in the ungrounded assumption that astrology requires belief in order to work. Astrology is not a philosophy or a religion unless we make it one. Astrology does not require my belief for it to work. *I don't believe in astrology; I use it because it works.* And it seems to work best as a language, not a belief system or a religion or a science. I also confess to not always knowing why or how it works. Astrology has a long history of mystery and argument around its actual workings.

3) Fortune Telling

Many people firmly believe that astrology and astrologers can predict the future. This regretful assumption classifies astrology as *fortune-telling*, further dismissing its integrity. Though I personally use astrological techniques called "Transits" to interpret certain forces at play, I am careful to frame my results as *tendencies*, not absolutes. I do not believe in this ridiculous Planets as Puppet Masters scenario based in the dogma that planets control our fates. I prefer to view planetary orbits as a measure of *the timing of change* but not their cause. I like to think the true causes of our fates may be far more complex and even mysterious (some may wish to study the astrology of fixed stars which this book won't go into). Take it from Joseph Campbell who once said, *"The best way to predict the future is to create it."*

4) The Entertainment Industry

Scripts written and produced in the Television and Film industries often feature astrologers as unreliable characters. "The Astrologer" is depicted as a kook or someone linked with supernatural powers which, in the business of commerce, usually sells itself to the public as terror or comedy. It's very rare that any supernatural or psychic phenomena is depicted in films or TV as a natural, positive, or ordinary function of the human psyche. Other times, The Astrologer is portrayed as a harmless, whimsical nobody, easily forgotten or even victimized. Astrologers as characters in Hollywood stories never seem to win.

5) Astrology Books

The sad truth is that too many astrology books are poorly written. There's this pervasive problem of redundancy (over-writing) and a compulsive need to "prove" astrology, as if to earn status points from more skeptical mainstream readers or maybe from absent fathers. Many astrology books are also written with little or no sense of humor or imagination, resulting in a dreary reading experience on a topic innately rich with colorful, dynamic mythological and archetypal correlations. Worst of all are those astrology books that posit their theories as dogmas or absolute beliefs. Exceptions to all of this dismal writing include the astrology books of Stephen Arroyo, Steven Forrest, Martin Schulman, Dane Rudhyar, Robert Hand, Liz Greene, and Jeffrey Wolf Green. And, of course, yours truly.

Though other sources of misinformation exist, these five appear to me as the most common assumptions and misunderstandings about astrology. As more students, teachers, and readers of the celestial language can bypass them, in lieu of more critical thinking and more poetic interpretations, perhaps the true value and purpose of the celestial language can be revived and sustained.

THE 12 SYMBOLIC SETS
Astrology as a Language of Associations

Forces, States and Styles:
The Planets, Houses and Signs Revisioned

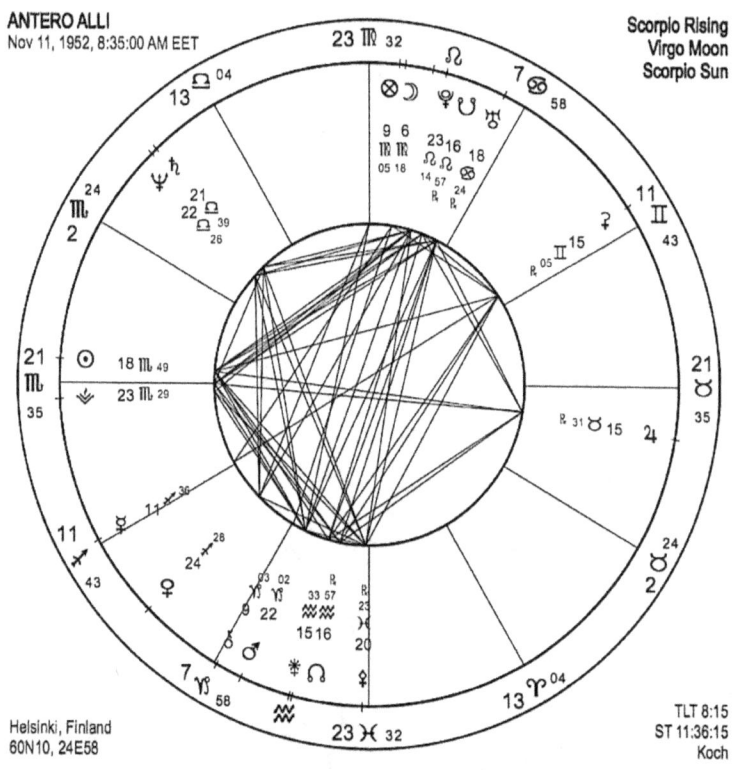

In the spirit of XA, throughout this book I will share a few of my real-life experiences and how I see them symbolized in my natal horoscope. Starting with the sign at the very bottom of the chart (aka the "nadir"), the 4th house cusp symbolizes the foundation of one's life, the personal support system, and how family and home might be experienced and defined.

Pisces at my nadir associates with Neptune and also the 12th house. Where are the clues? I look to the placement of Neptune and I find it in the 11th Community State conjunct Saturn. Since childhood, I've always felt more at home in the company of friends and later, with my theatre and filmmaking groups, than with my actual genetic family. I also feel little interest in researching my ancestry. For more clues, I look at the 12th house and there's my Scorpio Sun. I have come to realize how my sense of self has developed by the grace of these varied social experiences alongside a passion for withdrawal, solitude and contemplation.

In my 1990 book, *Astrologik* (and its 1999 revision), I changed three key astrological terms—*Houses, Planets, and Signs*—to "States, Forces and Styles," respectively. These semantic adjustments were made to support a more intuitive experience of the realities these terms represent. XA continues this direction through balancing the parallel paths of symbolic understanding of the horoscope with firsthand experiences of the real-life dynamics represented there. Overemphasize the symbolic and you can mistake the map for the territory. Overemphasize intuition and you can be at loss for words, failing to communicate what you alone may silently know.

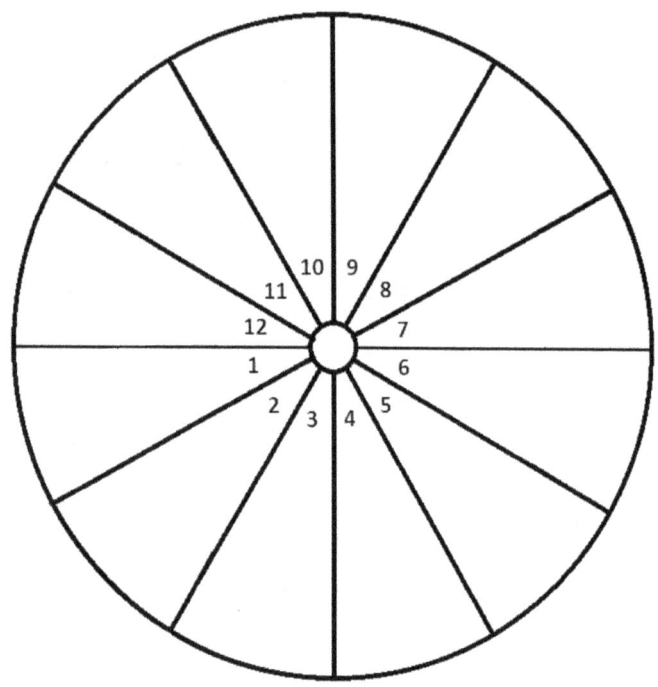

The States

1) State of Being
2) State of Survival
3) State of Mind
4) Sustaining State
5) Creative State
6) State of Employment
7) State of Intimacy
8) State of Surrender
9) State of Faith
10) Professional State
11) State of the Community
12) State of the Soul

Experiencing the States

The twelve houses of astrology refer to twelve different areas or states of human experience. Those who have lived more well-rounded lives may have greater access to most or all of these twelve states of experience, whether they know astrology or not. Those living more sheltered lives may have concentrated their life experiences into a third to two thirds of the twelve states, and may find difficulty grasping the meaning of states they have little to no experience with.

I like to think the best astrologers are living, or have lived, the most well-rounded lives. They are not just astrologers, but also artists, poets, mountain climbers, dancers, musicians, fathers and mothers, hospice workers, vintners, gardeners, etc. In this spirit, XA encourages expanding your real-life experience. As wonderful as this idea may seem to some, it may be one reason why this book may not be for everybody. Some individuals have legitimate reasons to remain cocooned in safer, more predictable and narrow lives. In my world, living life always comes first with astrology a close third behind Art.

Once a rudimentary grasp of the language of Forces, States and Styles can be achieved, it is possible to begin consciously experiencing these forces firsthand. This process starts with an understanding of the houses, or states, and the house cusps, or what I refer to as the *Governors* of each state in the United States of Yourself. I initially thought of renaming the house cusps "landlords" and "landladies" of each house but that didn't quite convey their true function as access points to each state. This governor idea is a subset of a greater framework of self-government, or sovereignty, this book is based on.

Every State Has a Governor

Using the map to find the territory means knowing how to gain access to the experiences symbolized by the state, or house, where entry is desired. Look at the style (sign) that starts each house as a direct entry point to the experience of that state. For example, a

Pisces 5th state Governor can indicate access to creative states through the *receptivity* necessary to be inspired. Someone with an Aries 5th state governor might access creative states more through instinct and visceral impulses of *excitement*. Aquarius on the 5th house cusp symbolizes the engagement of creative states through *teamwork or social dynamics*.

Though the planets (forces) within each state can obviously be active whether we consciously enter its state or not, the subjective experience of passing through the governor can amplify the experience. It's like the door to a room. You have to first open the door and walk into the room before meeting the inhabitants (the planets). Of course, the planets, and the energies they represent, can also be experienced without passing through the state governor. This happens with transits to our natal chart and also when the forces of other people act on our lives by shared aspects and synastries. The style governing each state serves as transition or bridge into that experience.

Each Force Casts a Shadow

The planetary glyphs in any chart represent dynamic forces at various degrees of latency, expression and manifestation. For example, Mercury represents the mental force of thinking and Mars, the visceral force of will. Just because these symbols exist in a chart does not necessarily mean they are consciously integrated yet. Forces often remain unintegrated by being neglected or exaggerated—which can distort their truer qualities. I look at this distortion as the "shadow aspect" of that force.

An overemphasized or exaggerated Mercury might manifest as over-thinking or anxiety. A repressed Mars might act out as the shadow of immobilizing passivity, indecision or apathy. Whether overemphasized or neglected, any given force seems to act out unconsciously in unbalanced ways as negative traits and destructive behaviors until recognized, accepted and integrated. When Mercury is integrated, we learn to think for ourselves. When Mars is integrated, we know what we want. The shadow aspect of each force (planet) will be covered in detail later in this Twelve Symbolic Sets section, along with examples of how integration might occur.

Styles Give Forces Color & Meaning

The twelve Astrological archetypes are presented as twelve *styles* of expression. They do not represent forces *per se,* but HOW a given force (planet) might be known to us. The States (or Houses) show us WHERE the energy dynamics of the Forces (planets) take place. The Forces show WHAT something is; the Styles show HOW a given force manifests through a specific State of experience.

The DNA of each of the 12 styles is made up of *one element, one modality, and a totem* (except for Scorpio which has many). The elements are Earth (sensation), Water (feeling), Fire (intuition), and Air (thinking). The three modalities are Fixed (concentrating), Mutable (circulating) and Cardinal (radiating).

For example, Scorpio is Fixed Water: concentrating the feeling mode creates passion. Capricorn is Cardinal Earth: radiating sensation manifests materiality. Gemini is Mutable Air: circulating mental associations. All 12 Styles convey characteristics innate to their traditional totems as: *creatures* (Aries the Ram, Taurus the Bull, Cancer the Crab, Leo the Lion, Scorpio the Scorpion, Sagittarius the Centaur, Capricorn the Goat, Pisces the Fishes), *humans* (Gemini the Twins, Virgo the Virgin, Aquarius the Water Bearer), and *an object* (Libra; the scales of justice). When any style becomes over-emphasized or neglected, it can also distort into its shadow aspect.

Integration of and by the Forces

Throughout this book references are made to the idea of *integrating* this force, or being *integrated by* that force. The personal forces—*Sun, Moon, Mercury, Venus, Mars, Jupiter and Saturn*—symbolize specific forces within the developing personality corresponding to sense of identity, feelings and habits, thoughts and theories, likes and dislikes, excitements and actions, beliefs and responsibilities. The personal forces express a spectrum of personal reactions to life, to whatever happens—each with its own distinct force, or energy. Our capacity for having an experience determines the capacity for its integration. Whatever can be fully experienced can be fully integrated. Forces that can be integrated become embodied in us as memory and energy, as image and feeling—no longer abstractions or symbols on a screen or a page.

The transpersonal forces—*Uranus, Neptune and Pluto*—symbolize *impersonal archetypes* that subject the personality to more objective truths such as innate autonomy, cosmic unity, and impermanence. We do not integrate these transpersonal forces as much as we can become integrated *by them*. Through Uranus, we awaken to our sovereignty after recognizing oppression. Through Neptune, we face suffering before learning compassion, and through Pluto, we enter the eternal cycles of death and rebirth and to better endure life's many changes and rites of passage. As we are integrated by these transpersonal agencies, the thread of our personal lives are woven into the universal tapestry of the collective, the world, the universe.

Activating the Forces

I used to believe I could control my emotions, thoughts, impulses, infatuations, perceptions and fears. But in truth, emotions (Moon), thoughts (Mercury), visceral impulses and desires (Mars), feelings of love (Venus), perceptions (Jupiter), fears (Saturn) are *autonomous*. They have lives of their own beyond my control.

Applying certain ritual methods, I began experimenting with a more conscious activation of the forces symbolized in my chart as the planets. It soon became clear that these forces could not be approached directly without contriving the results. Through repeated experiments, I discovered how these autonomous forces became activated *indirectly* by first engaging the experiences innate to their respective houses. To activate these forces, I simply had to find ways to first fully engage those experiences. For example: by subjecting myself to more 11th house group and social experiences, the forces symbolized by my Saturn/Neptune conjunction immediately availed themselves.

Interpreting astrology charts can feel a bit like detective work. Horoscopes must be examined for clues to the potentialities someone might've been born with, how they might go about realizing them, and any obstacles that need to be identified before they can be overcome. This clue-gathering process depends on knowing which planets are associated with which signs and houses in their own symbolic set, or family. Each of the following twelve sections outline these astrological sets. Three planets—*Mercury, Venus* and *Mars*—have dual residencies as each one belongs to two different sets or families. Mercury appears with Virgo and the 6th house, as well as with Gemini and the 3rd house. Venus makes her home with Taurus and the 2nd house when she's not with Libra and the 7th house. Mars kicks it with Aries in the 1st house and also with Pluto and Scorpio in the 8th house. These differences will be explained as we go.

Aries, Mars, 1st House
(State of Being), and the Ascendant

ARIES; Cardinal Fire (A Bonfire)

A Fighter archetype, the bold style of Aries symbolizes the spark of excitability seeking immediate expression and action. Cardinal Fire, the source of the powers of heat and luminosity, Aries refers to the instinctive, visceral response to sensory stimuli as impulse and a push for action. The RAM charges; Aries represents where we may love being in charge and making choices. As the first sign in the zodiac, Aries expresses a "me first" energy, not because it's selfish in a negative way. Like a sprout breaking ground to open air on the first day of Spring, Aries symbolizes the primal vital rush of life itself.

ARIES Shadow: pushy, over-controlling, vain, combative

The ARIES Governor, or House Cusp

Whatever state Aries governs points to where the entire chart and the entire life start. It's a defining point that can indicate where and how we *self-identify*. This can be where a desire for excitement and being in control defines the experience of the state. There can be a healthy need for single-handedly taking charge of the experience where Aries governs. Since real life situations are mostly not under personal control, this may be a safe place to satiate the desire for asserting will and having things go our own way. When this need for control is frustrated, it can run rampant across the map in nonstop control trips over whatever and whomever cannot actually be controlled. Aries itself is not "a controlling sign" *per se* but as a governor it can indicate where the need for control can be fulfilled safely.

Aries Cusp Examples

4: family- or clan-identified, domestic territoriality
5: creative control, artist-identified, adventurous
6: self-employment, work-identified, quality control
9: philosophically-defined, identified by one's beliefs
12: achieving control by withdrawal, escape into solitude

MARS, a Visceral Force of Will and Excitement

The Warrior spirit of Mars acts from the source of whatever genuinely excites us. It's that simple and direct. Look to Mars' style and state for indications of a personal excitement criteria. For example, Mars in the First State of Being can indicate a self-starter where self-motivation requires no assistance to get going. Those with a 3rd state Mars might be excited by ideas. Someone with a 7th state Mars might be motivated by doing things for the partner.

Mars symbolizes how we can raise enough physical energy to get things done. Mars, "the Doer", the Actor, is motivated by personal drives, excitements and thrills. Mars' visceral force of excitement naturally arouses the personal will to power and self-confidence. Knowing what excites you can show you what you want. Mars symbolizes territorial instincts and its natal placement can indicate a push for expanding the turf and the desire to control the area represented by the state (house) Mars is in.

Aspect Notes

When Mars shares aspects with the transpersonal forces of Uranus, Neptune or Pluto, there can be a strident drive to do great things or, perhaps, to join the combined thrills of many others towards collective action. The archetype of the Warrior may be guiding the inner psychic life. Personal planets (Sun to Saturn) aspected by Mars tend to express themselves more actively and forcefully. Mars activates.

The Shadow of Mars

A frustrated Mars can act out in at least two ways: *overly active and overly passive*. An overly passive Mars can appear as indecisiveness, timidity, apathy and a reluctance to take action. This can result from being out of touch with what actually excites us or turns us on. We may become passive victims of circumstance, unwilling and unable to make decisions, defend ourselves, or fight for what matters.

On the other extreme, an overactive Mars can result in overdoing, pushy and controlling behavior, trying too hard, bullying others, and a forceful resentment when we're not getting our way: Mars the Brat. The result of overdoing can also cast a kind of psychic shielding, or ego armor, inhibiting the receptivity for relating more honestly and openly with others.

ASCENDANT (aka Rising Sign, 1st House cusp)

The horizontal line across any chart represents the horizon at the time and place of birth. The sign at the far left of this horizontal line is the Rising Sign (aka Ascendant). It's called the Rising Sign, or Ascendant, because this sign represents the specific constellation that was ascending over the horizon at the time and place of birth. The Ascendant characterizes a person by their overall approach to life that can be identified by the Rising sign.

The qualities of each Rising Sign become more obvious when awareness aligns with the present moment and with the body that is always in present time. A sense of personhood, of what is most personal to us and about us, develops as we inhabit the present. As we do this, we show up and our personal presence becomes known to us and others through the filter of the Rising Sign. Personhood does not means any self-image or mask or persona, but an instinctive sense of one's own energy and presence in the unfolding moment. The Rising Sign represents the most present-time sensitive point on the chart and our most immediate instinctive reactions to whatever happens to us.

When I need insight on behavioral issues—like "acting out," "attitudes," or "posturing"—I look to the Rising Sign. I also try to see if the client has become overly preoccupied with the past or the future and lost touch with who they are in the present. Each of the twelve signs conveys a distinct style of self-expression, behavior and instinctive ways we move through the world and even how we enter a room. In the world of physical theatre and dance, the Rising Sign can be recognized as a *movement signature*.

1st HOUSE—STATE OF BEING

Body & Five Senses, Behavior, Personal Energy

The State of Being represents how we behave, what characterizes us, and what sets us apart from others. We instinctively embody whatever forces reside in this state, and experience them as they act out through us. First House experience is not planned or contrived as much as a direct expression of qualities symbolized by the Rising Sign and any forces in the State of Being. Here we experience our consciousness through The Body and the five senses. The Rising Sign and any forces residing in this state give rise to the character we are in our own movie, how we experience ourselves, and also how we're seen by others. The State of Being and the Rising Sign convey qualities and attributes defining what is most personal about us. What could be more personal than how you experience your consciousness through the Body, and how that acts out in your behavior?

Balance Point (7th House)

As the sense of selfhood and individual integrity increases, we may be more ready for the interpersonal challenges in the 7th State of Intimacy. When we become too full of ourselves or too self-centered, balance can be restored by initiating relationships and sharing our life with another.

**Taurus, Venus, 2nd House
(State of Survival)**

TAURUS; Fixed Earth (A Robust Garden)

Taurus, a Builder archetype, harkens back to when the Great Pyramids were built with immeasurable patience and persistence five thousand years ago during the peak of the Age of Taurus (3000 BCE). Fixed Earth, the *concentration of sensation,* refers to a strong focus in the material dimension. Taurus represents a stabilizing influence to whatever force passes through it, slowing it down through *the sphere of sensation.* Taurus the BULL never rushes but takes its time, sits patiently, and knows its place. Taurean slowness does not indicate any lack of intelligence, but an innate need for *thoroughness* to evaluate and establish the worthiness of a thing, a situation, a person, or an experience. Taurean qualities of loyalty, consistency, persistence and stubbornness stem from this notion that once true value is established, there's little need to change anything. Taurus represents integration, of making something one's own, that sense of ownership arising when something has been truly earned.

TAURUS Shadow: bull-headed, lazy, overly territorial

The TAURUS Governor, or House Cusp

Whatever state Taurus governs symbolizes an area where we may need to slow down and simplify to discover the true value of the experience in that state. It's where trust in the experience may need to be earned and built over time. It can also be where consistency, loyalty and a stabilizing influence may be necessary to evaluate what is worthwhile and what is worthless. Whatever state Taurus governs indicates where and how we define *security and status, and* what makes us feel stable and worthy. In Taurus' state we can, or may need to, experience increasing degrees of *havingness,* that sense of gratitude for what we already have.

Taurus Cusp Examples

3: slower learning to be more thorough
5: body– and sensation-based creativity

9: finding value in one's point of view and beliefs
11: a need for stability and loyalty in friendships

VENUS, a Magnetic Force of Attraction

Though Venus belongs to both Taurus and Libra, its Taurean spirit aligns more with sensuality and an aesthetic appreciation for material possessions of beauty and decor. This Venus also shows a knack for finance and finesse with business negotiations. Venus symbolizes the sensations of attraction, affection and love—whether for fine material things or individuals we find attractive. Above all, Venus refers to *relational social intelligence,* of how well we interact and get along with others. What and who is worthy of your heart? For Venus, interpersonal relationships are sustained by the value each person invests and derives from the experience with another.

In some relationships, one person acts as the Holder of Value for the other(s). Other relationships are sustained by shared values. Conflicting values between partners may be one of the more common causes of breakups. When navigating our lives by the on/off switch of *what we like and dislike*, we are guided by Venus. If most or all our choices are based on whether or not we like or dislike something or someone, Venus turns tyrannical and obscures other equally valid ways to assess any situation or person beyond the subjectivity of personal likes and dislikes. *The Petulant Venus.*

Aspect Notes

When Venus shares aspects with the transpersonal forces of Uranus, Neptune or Pluto, there can arise a longing for a higher love in relationships or marriages that don't conform to consensus reality standards of romance. The archetype of a Goddess may be guiding one's inner psychic life. When Venus aspects other personal forces, they become harmonized with pleasant, charismatic and appealing qualities. Venus charms.

The Shadow of Venus (Taurus Aspect)

An over-emphasized Venus can play out as languishing passivity, or a sense of being intoxicated or drunk on one's own beauty and aesthetics. This can lead to imposing personal values and aesthetic standards onto others. Any pursuit of Venusian pleasure and beauty above all else can overwhelm other dimensions of life—*duty, work, family, intellectual development, friendships*—and run Venus ragged to the bone.

In its extreme, too much Venus can appear as the kind of procrastination that comes from waiting for things to magically happen all by themselves—like in a fairytale. An underdeveloped Venus can act out as lower social intelligence, a lack of personal taste and aesthetics, a disregard for one's appearance and an ambivalence for what is worth liking or loving. In extreme *Venus disconnect* we can lose heart, or cannot find beauty anywhere; or perhaps fail to appreciate what we have by constantly wanting what we cannot have.

2nd HOUSE—STATE OF SURVIVAL
Values, Self-Worth, The Bank of the Chart

What is it that makes your life worth living, without which your life might not be worth living? Look to the sign (the Governor) ruling this State and any planets residing here for clues. The State of Survival refers to how we stay alive, earn income and define our values to maintain a sense of self-worth in an impersonal world. Planets here can define the dynamics of our value system. With Uranus, personal and financial independence can make a life worth living. With Venus, a constant source of love, beauty and art makes life worth living. With 2nd house Neptune, following a dream makes life worth living. More than two planets in the State of Survival represents a complex value system as well as a greater sense of resourcefulness, like having more money in the bank.

The 2nd house is like the Bank of the chart. State of Survival planets symbolize our personal resources and the kind of currency we trade in. This could be money or real estate. but it can also be a wealth of skills, knowledge, talent, art, love, friends and power; currency comes in many forms. When we discover what makes our lives worth living, our survival agendas and income-generating processes can become more aligned with our values. When this happens, self-worth increases. When our income-generating jobs are not aligned with our core values, self-worth diminishes.

As we discover how true value is defined and known, it is only natural to hold onto it. It's hard to let go of a sure thing when that's also a good thing. As a result, the State of Survival shows us where and what we become most tenacious about, especially if it was earned.

Balance Point (8th House)

When we become overly-entrenched in our own survival agendas, values and security needs, 8th house experiences can push us past our comfort zones by enough meaningful change to accelerate personal development and growth. These transformative experiences may require release of the monkey grip on our security agendas and needs.

Gemini, Mercury, 3rd House
(State of Mind)

Experiential Astrology

GEMINI; Mutable Air (A High-Powered Antenna)

Gemini, a Messenger archetype, refers to mental processes of translating experiences into labels, meanings and narratives. As a Mutable Air style, its highly interactive, mobilizing influence circulates and distributes the dynamics within any planet or force. Like an antenna or a radar disk, Gemini constantly interprets raw signals into messages, words, language. Its totem, THE TWINS, represents the dualistic dimension of a mind given to free-association of ideas, comparing one thing with another, finding new combinations and hybrids along the way. The fine-tuned, detail-oriented Gemini style remains in motion like the wind spreading seeds across the land. A *puer aeternus* spirit pervades Gemini's endless curiosity to learn whatever it can about the immediate local environment.

GEMINI *Shadow: scattered, superficial, distracted, petty*

The GEMINI Governor, or House Cusp

Whatever state Gemini governs symbolizes a need for greater variety and mental stimulation. It can be where gathering data satiates an ongoing curiosity about the experience. The accumulation of preconceptions in this state can sometimes stir a sense of *ambiguity* around the experience. The Gemini house cusp can show us where options are necessary to stay interested, engaged and open to the ever-increasing influx of new information. Gemini creates plans and maps on how to navigate the experience.

Gemini Cusp Examples

4: at home living in the domain of mind; dual residency
6: "jack of all trades, master of none"; many job skills
8: endless curiosity about sexual experience
11: diversity of social life; "social butterfly"

MERCURY, a Mental Force of Thinking

Though Mercury belongs with both Gemini and Virgo, the Gemini spirit expresses an intellectual capacity for thinking and generating theories, preconceptions, and agendas. Thinking is not the same as being logical; logic follows specific Aristotelian laws. The thinking "mind" of this Mercury orients around solving mundane problems, making sense of things by naming and labeling sensory input. To this Gemini mind, *interpretation is everything*—automatically assigning meaning, names, and labels to whatever can be perceived. Our world is conceptualized by how we think, talk, and write about it. Whatever sign Mercury is in conveys something of our *intellectual style* and *how we process information*. When interpretations and preconceptions are confused for actual experience, the map is mistaken for the territory and real life starts slipping away unnoticed.

Aspect Notes

When Mercury shares aspects with the transpersonal forces of Uranus, Neptune or Pluto, there can be a marked amplification of thought processes pushing the thinking mind beyond herd mentality to think outside that box. The archetype of the god Hermes may be guiding the inner psychic life. When Mercury aspects personal forces, thinking processes are colored and shaped by their influences. Mercury verbalizes.

The Shadow of Mercury (Gemini Aspect)

An overemphasized Mercury can play out as over-thinking, second-guessing and the anxiety from mental entanglement in too many ideas and preconceptions. When theories fail to be tested in repeat experiments, they can assume a kind of paper-tiger authority without evidence or proof. When over-identified with intellect, the mind can turn into a thinking machine with no "off" switch. A neglected, or "unintegrated," Mercury can parrot the ideas of others due to a lack of creative thought. This can indicate an insecurity or shame around not being smart or smart enough.

Lack of intellectual development can also appear as an inclination to generalize and exaggerate, or as the kind of *formulaic thinking* characterized by an excessive use of the word "is" (in mathematical formulas, the equal sign "=" mirrors the word "is"). Formulaic thinking can produce overly-literalist and dogmatic speech patterns as well as writing and thinking styles—all anathema to creative thought and imagination.

3rd HOUSE—STATE OF MIND

Learning, Speaking, Writing, & Communicating

The 3rd House cusp can indicate our "learning style," how we might most effectively educate ourselves, solve problems, interpret and communicate our ideas, make maps of our experiences and share them with others. Planets (forces) residing here act as "filters" shaping how we think, talk and write. 3rd House Neptune might convey a daydreaming mind with an imaginative thinking process. Venus in the State of Mind can indicate an attraction to ideas we feel the most affection or love for, while disregarding the rest. 3rd House Sun individuals may learn best when education becomes self-referential. Forces in the State of Mind require stimulation, interaction and learning experiences to develop. The 3rd House represents the ideational, blueprinting, and planning stages of any given project, but not usually how they can be engineered or manifested in the world.

Balance Point (9th House)

When over-identification with the thinking machine ensnares us with too many concepts, labels, details and nonstop data-gathering, we can find balance in 9th house Big Picture experiences that expand our consciousness: travel, culture shock, psychoactive drug trips, and vision quests. As we reach beyond the familiar, more reality can be perceived giving rise to fresh perspectives.

Cancer, the Moon, 4th House (Sustaining State), and the Nadir

CANCER; Cardinal Water (A Wellspring)

Cancer, a Caretaker archetype, deepens the subjective experience of what is worth caring about. Cardinal Water refers to the outpouring source of the powers of life-giving, nourishing experiences. Cancer's totem, the CRAB, has powerful claws and a hard shell showing great tenacity and protection of a sensitive inner life. There's a mother within everyone, and all mothers are defined by the children they feed, care for, and raise—whether that's genetic children, pets, house plants, or creative projects. The Cancer archetype symbolizes the internal trinity of the Mother, Infant and Child Within and any living thing that needs *protection and nurturance to survive*.

CANCER Shadow: *worrisome, defensive, smothering*

The CANCER Governor, or House Cusp

Cancer symbolizes where we are emotionally invested or, perhaps, need to be. This house cusp shows us what we may genuinely care about, or maybe should be caring about. Whether it's for our art or children (5th house), sacred beliefs (9th house), money (2nd house), or domestic life (4th house), Cancer points to where we become emotionally attached, whether we are aware of it or not. Sometimes, it can be easy to overlook how attached we have become as emotions run deep in the Subconscious. The state Cancer governs points to an area where we experience a *sustaining care*; whatever we nurture, nurtures us in return. We can be emotionally sustained by the experience of the state Cancer governs. Whenever this area is judged or criticized by others, we can feel attacked, offended or have "hurt feelings" and react defensively: claws out!

Cancer Cusp Examples

2: family values, security as fulfillment and happiness
5: sustained by creative states, emotion-based art
7: attracted to a nurturing mate or mother figure
11: making friends as family, strong social bonds

THE MOON, an Emotional Force of Habit & Need

The Moon symbolizes biological, instinctive needs for comfort, shelter and contentment. When these needs are denied, our lives become overly complicated with emotional frustration and discontent. When we lose touch with the Moon, depression can eventually set in, alerting us to an emotional disconnect. (Depression is not the same as sorrow or grief which are lively in comparison.) The natal placement of the Moon can indicate where (the state) and how (the style) we can restore a sense of safety and comfort when we're feeling anxious, stressed or traumatized. The 12th house Moon offers comfort through retreat and solitude. Taurus Moon can self-soothe with comfort food. Virgo Moon persons can calm down simply by making themselves useful.

Each Moon sign defines familiarity and a sense of safety in subjective ways; one person's safety can be another person's danger. We are a clinging species and our natal Moon remains a soulful reminder of our personal needs and animal nature—*how we depend on others and are also just like everybody else.* The Moon's natal placement points to an area where emotional investment and attachment occurs, whether it's wanted or not. The Moon sign symbolizes the *emotional style* of how we process emotional reactions to daily pressures, problems and successes. Gemini Moons get chatty, Sagittarius Moons get high, Aquarius Moons throw a party.

The Moon symbolizes the first force to be activated in our lives as *totally dependent infants.* The Moon also represents the depository of all life experiences stored as memory in the Body/Psyche; memory moon. Contrary to popular astrology columns, we may be far more akin to our Moon sign than our Sun sign. The Sun points more to who *we are becoming,* whereas the Moon shows more of who we have already become through our personal history.

Many, but not all, of our emotional issues stem from how a mother, whether genetic or surrogate, raised us. The Moon's sign and house can sometimes tell us about the mother. My 9th house Virgo Moon is a pretty good symbol for a working mom who travelled. I find comfort in the work I do and, though I don't travel extensively, I do explore a rather wild spectrum of metaphysical interests. *Thanks mom!*

Aspect Notes

When the Moon shares aspects with the transpersonal forces of Uranus, Neptune or Pluto, there can be a deeper felt sense of collective shifts of the era, as well as empathy for collective suffering, where the pain felt may not be entirely one's own. The archetype of the Great Mother may be guiding the inner psychic life. When the Moon aspects other personal forces, they become infused by the subjective influences of emotional truths and memory. The Moon deepens.

The Shadow of the Moon

When the Moon becomes exalted over other forces in our nature, we can feel more owned by *the force of habit,* a common enough occurrence. This can happen when we are convinced that we need far more comfort and security than may actually be necessary. If our comfort zones are not balanced by periodic challenges and new experiences, emotional stagnation can set in and stunt personal growth. Live too much for your Moon and everyday life can become like an insular cocoon of inertia. *There's a fine line between a rut and a groove.*

When the Moon is under-emphasized, there can be a loss of what brings real satisfaction. This loss can also lead to a lack of connectivity and bonding with others. Despair, depression, a disconnect from support systems can also be symptoms of lunar disconnect. Losing the Moon can be a down-and-out place to be.

THE NADIR (4th House Cusp)

The 4th House cusp is called the Nadir, meaning "the bottom." This sign, or style, can reveal clues to what sustains us emotionally and how comfort, satisfaction and self-nurturing can be felt and even defined. The Nadir's sign can also represent a geomantic sensitivity for the kind of bioregion we most naturally feel at home in: Pisces by the sea, Sagittarius or Capricorn on the mountain, Taurus in the valley, etc. The Nadir articulates our innermost self that only those who live with us every day can know about since our most private selves are rarely displayed on the impersonal world stage—unless we're fearless, exhibitionistic, performing artists. The Nadir can also point to the ancestral legacies of moral codes passed down through the generations, those rules of conduct that define what "the Smiths" do and don't do. Break the family rules and risk clan or tribal banishment.

4th HOUSE—SUSTAINING STATE

Home & Family, Support Systems, Lifestyle

Perhaps the most complex of all twelve states, Fourth house experience embraces a deep webbing of ancestral legacies, family bonds, childhood traumas, and psychological and moral conditioning. Though 4th house is traditionally linked with home and family; not all families and homes offer sustenance, comfort and support to the naturally needy child. The underlying essence of this house speaks to the kind of support system each person may have been raised with or experienced a lack thereof. Support systems amount to whatever or whomever may be necessary to endure the pressures of daily life.

Planets residing here can symbolize character traits (and sometimes genetic diseases) inherited from ancestors, clan-defining moral codes passed down through generations, and other unconscious forces only made conscious and integrated after becoming our own parents—not just as literal parents, but by becoming fully accountable for our own needs. The Sustaining State can indicate how we domesticate and what kind of life we need to be living—our lifestyle—to support the realization of our dreams, goals and public ambitions. *Who and what can be depended on when we're down and out?*

The Sustaining State refers to a very private place of how we domesticate (or not), and how we make a home for ourselves to sustain our lives. This area can also indicate domestic compatibility and/or strife with other household members (family or friends). Typically, those sharing Nadir signs in the same element (*Fire, Earth, Water* or *Air*) tend to harmonize, whereas those sharing squared signs at their Nadir can sometimes become more domestically quarrelsome, i.e., *Leo/Scorpio, Aries/Capricorn, Taurus/Aquarius, etc.* Of course, there are always exceptions and other factors to be examined for how people can effectively share the same home.

Balance Point (10th House)

When we have become excessively domesticated, live overly sheltered lives, or feel trapped by family guilt complexes, we can find balance by clarifying our own 10th house goals and ambitions, and then pursuing them to establish our own identity, our own vision, and our own voice. Sometimes, in doing so, conflicts can arise with family or clan members who feel threatened by any experiences defined as *taboo* by that family or clan's moral code. The root of these moral conflicts may run deep into ancestral family feuds with rebellious offspring—the "black sheep"—who may be acting as frontier scouts for their gene pool—launching far from the familial hub to the outer limits of high novelty, pushing the evolutionary envelope for their family.

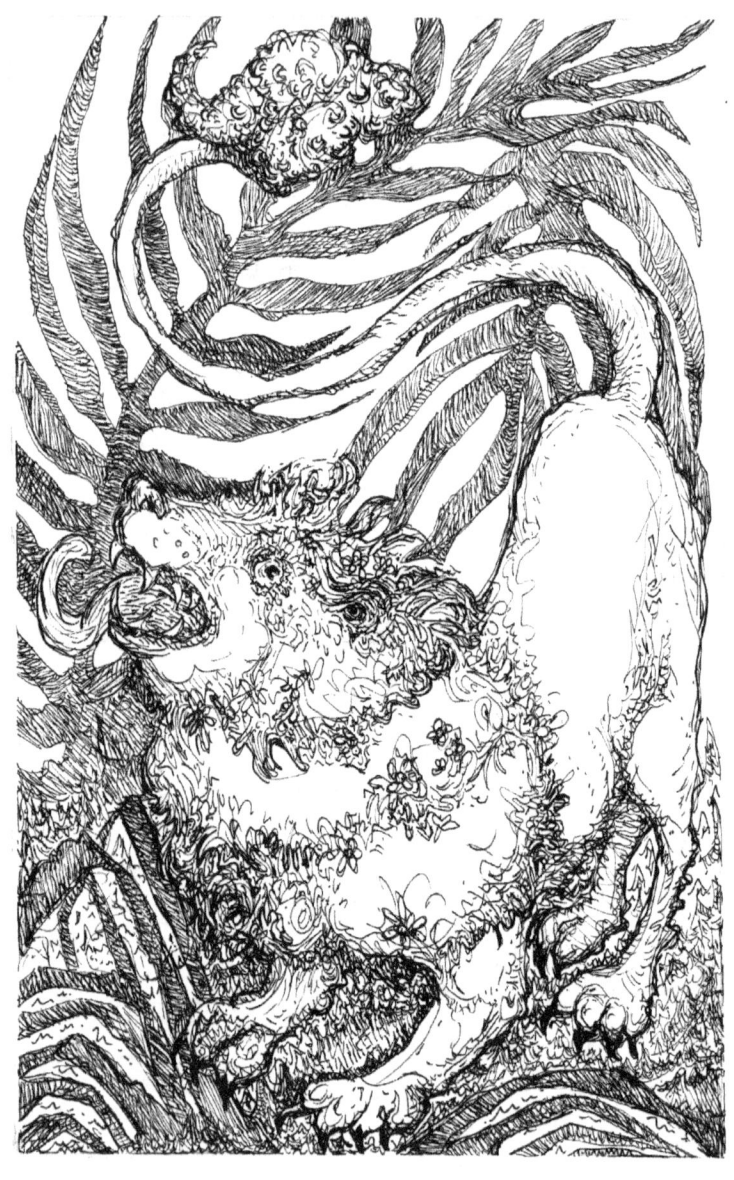

Leo, the Sun, 5th House
(Creative State)

LEO; Fixed Fire (A Welding Torch)

Leo, a Magical Child archetype. The element of Fixed Fire concentrates intuitive experience in the vital life force and the frequency of energy within any given situation. Leo's playful style enlivens existence with creative impulses and an arousing pleasure and joy for entertaining ourselves and others. With or without an audience, Leo represents a performative spirit for creating a world of its own and the enchantment of inhabiting that world *with the seriousness of a child at play*. Leo's totem, the LION, "King of the Beasts," shows a desire to dominate the scene, be adored and applauded—sometimes for ego, other times for its creations. Like the Sun it represents, Leo's native generosity of warmth can sometimes give far more of itself than it may know how to receive.

LEO Shadow: narcissistic, excessive pride, self-absorbed

The LEO Governor, or House Cusp

Whatever State Leo governs symbolizes an area of our lives where we do well to have more fun, be more creative, and discover more joy. Sometimes these states indicate hidden talents where a more improvisational approach can be more effective than "going by the book" or following a formula or plan. The Leo state can sometimes be characterized by experiences seeking an audience or a stage, figuratively if not literally. Exhibitionistic tendencies may also arise in this state, as well as a genuine spirit of generosity, warmth and charisma.

Leo Cusp Examples

3: learns best in a spirit of play; story-telling style
7: attracted to charismatic creative types
8: can be sexually generous with the partner
11: artists as friends, creating group projects, play pals

THE SUN, a Self-Realizing Force of Becoming

The Sun symbolizes a King or Queen, a Leader-spirit radiating a depth of warmth and luminosity. The Sun shows us where (house) and how (sign) we shine when the Sun is not obscured or obstructed by clouds. The Sun sign and house indicates how we can become as a star, *a shining entity*, given our potential and motivation for self-realization. Although almost everybody knows their Sun sign, not everyone has the energy and will to become as self-realizing stars. Those who do not care to self-realize, or are perhaps slower to realize themselves, may appear socially as satellites or "moons" revolving around more self-realizing stars, even happily so. Self-realizing stars perform well as the center of their posse or gang.

Feeding the Being

Whereas Mars represents "The Doer", the Sun expresses "The Being". Self-realization is nurtured by *feeding the being*. The being is fed by absorbing the essences of experiences innate to the state and style the Sun is in. A 10th house Cancer Sun person feeds the being by achieving goals based in what they care most about. Someone with a 5th house Taurus Sun might feed the being by getting paid for creating art. Those with a 12th house Libra Sun feed the being through solitary experiences in Nature that sustains their inner spiritual lives. The Sun eats experiences symbolized by its sign, house placements and aspects with other planets.

Self-realization (not to be confused with any final "enlightenment" or "spiritual arrival") persists in an ongoing process of self-work. This work demands a kind of *radical self-acceptance* for acknowledging what might be the worst and the best, the darkest and the brightest sides, of our Sun sign. A positive/negative polarity within every Sun acts like a power-generating psychic battery. By accepting and embracing the contrary forces of the Sun's nature, of our own being—*the good and the bad, the brilliance and the ignorance, the strengths and the weaknesses*—self-realizing individuals start generating more solar power of warmth and luminosity.

Others may feel and see this presence as *charisma*, an elusive quality that ignites a sense in others of feeling more open to being themselves around this person.

Some Examples of Sun Sign Polarities

Aries (bossy/spontaneous)
Taurus (stubborn/loyal)
Gemini (scattered/curious)
Cancer (smothering/nurturing)
Leo (vain/generous)
Virgo (over-critical/skillful)
Libra (indecisive/fair-minded)
Scorpio (controlling/authentic)
Sagittarius (evasive/direct)
Capricorn (laconic/dignified)
Aquarius (insolent/innovative)
Pisces (limp/inspired)

Aspect Notes

When the Sun shares aspects with the transpersonal forces of Uranus, Neptune or Pluto, there can be an identification with the "universal we" and an orientation to social or political causes to fight for and live by. The archetype of the Hero may be guiding the inner psychic life. When The Sun aspects other personal forces, the sense of identity is shaped and influenced by them. The Sun identifies.

The Shadow of the Sun

When the Sun sign becomes over-emphasized, narcissism can take root and if it continues, empathy for others diminishes. The "big Sun" person becomes blind to the influence of their own energy on others and can start acting as if consequences don't exist or no longer matter. In its extreme, sociopathic tendencies develop, alienating others and/or attracting those of lesser will to be victimized by the overbearing ego of the big Sun person. The neglected Sun can appear as a weak ego, as an ongoing identity crisis and/or an ongoing sense of not being taken seriously enough.

The degree our energy field, or aura, lacks illumination and warmth may be the degree we are out of touch with the Sun and those experiences that feed the being. We might start feeling invisible, as if we don't exist, and become as "non-entities" to ourselves and those we encounter. We may get caught in the futility trap of constantly comparing ourselves to everyone else. After realizing our uniqueness, these kinds of insecurities become irrelevant.

"Be yourself; everyone else is already taken." — *Oscar Wilde*

5th HOUSE—CREATIVE STATE

Pleasure & Joy, Adventure & Entertainment

The 5th house defines our unique *entertainment criteria*, what brings us joy and what is worth celebrating. Traditionally related to art, romance, adventure and children, the essence of 5th house experience belongs to the enchantment of the Inner Child archetype—who we were and still are deep inside, as children creating worlds to inhabit. This state can also indicate a propensity to bear offspring and relate with the Inner Child through raising genetic offspring.

Any forces here can be activated by entering a creative state; some forces can also symbolize artistic talents. Each of us approaches this area differently, symbolized by the style governing the Creative State. When Taurus governs the 5th house, creativity may be accessed through the body, as with dance, and maybe a bit slow to assure thoroughness. If Cancer governs the 5th house, a more feeling-based approach may stimulate creativity with an emotional focus on what is worth caring about and worth creating.

When the transpersonal forces of Uranus, Neptune and/or Pluto appear in the Creative state, either natally or by transit, they can represent *the Muses archetypes* inspiring creation. Not to be confused with "my" Muse or "your" Muse, these transpersonal forces refer to autonomous archetypes beyond ego. To the Muses, we are not "creators" as much as *vessels* expressing creative forces *through us*. When this basic truth is ignored, ego pride can inflate with exaggerated self-importance and creative channels shut down—easy to overlook when you're having too much fun. Transpersonal forces in the Creative State are not subject to our personal process of integration. They cannot be owned; more likely, the human vessels and artists are owned by them.

Balance Point (11th House)

When we have become overly enamored with ourselves or feel trapped in the naive bubble of our own worlds, we can find balance by entering 11th house social experiences of making friends and participating in community projects to discover a larger context than our own personal world. You are special and so is everyone else.

Virgo, Mercury, 6th House
(State of Employment)

VIRGO; Mutable Earth (A Farming Plough)

Virgo, a Harvest archetype, symbolizes a comprehensive and organized labor force that feeds the village. Mutable Earth distributes and circulates materiality in service to those in need. Like the agricultural process of separating wheat from the chaff, Virgo the Virgin attunes itself to what is good and pure, and disposes what is contaminated and corrupt. Morally, this represents the virtue of a pure heart. Psychologically, this correlates with discernment, analysis and the compartmentalization of putting things or ideas or feelings in their right places. Spiritually, the Virgin moves with humility in a spirit of service. Virgo keeps things in order, and values quality over quantity. All these attributes express the essence of Virgo that can, like any essence, become distorted by over-emphasis. Virgo distorts through anxiety, nitpicking, criticality, a superiority complex (snobbery), and the paralysis of analysis. The Virgo style imposes an organizing principle, or system, to arrange the chaos of life into its own kind of order. Virgo favors everything in its right place.

VIRGO Shadow: fussy, anxious, overly critical, snobby

The VIRGO Governor, or House Cusp

Virgo symbolizes where we may need a sense of order and organization to fully appreciate the experiences symbolized by whatever state it governs. There can be an inclination to use new tools and technology to navigate and improve the experience. The Virgo governor points to an area where quality matters. Quality control may be defined by work practices that optimally serve the situation at hand. This area can benefit from compartmentalization when managing different work projects at the same time. Intellectual properties of discernment, analysis, and criticism may also prevail here.

Virgo Cusp Examples

3: a prepared and organized approach to education

4: comfortable working at home
8: evolving oneself through new skills and methods
12: finding a sense of order in solitude and retreat

MERCURY, a Mental Force of Thinking

Though Mercury belongs to both Gemini and Virgo, the Virgo spirit sides more with the intellectual capacity for figuring out the mechanics of how things work and how theory gets put into practice. This intellect takes on a more practical role in problem-solving with a focus on solutions. The Virgo side of Mercury orients within a *work ethic* for how to best engineer a blueprint or plan into manifestation and *doing it the right way*. Unlike the Gemini side of Mercury, Virgo does not busy itself with constant associations between things, but with reasoning, logic and critical thinking. Organizing what has been gathered can be prioritized over constantly gathering data.

Aspect Notes

When Mercury shares aspects with the transpersonal forces of Uranus, Neptune or Pluto, there can be an acceleration of thought processes fueling increased activity in that state. The archetype of the Apprentice, or Servant, may be guiding the inner psychic life. When Mercury shares aspects with the other personal forces, it infuses them with a mental dimension of thinking, analysis or articulation. This Mercury is busy.

The Shadow of Mercury (Virgo Aspect)

An overemphasized Mercury can act out as exaggerated worry and an excessive fretting over imperfections, untidiness, disarray and incompetence. A kind of *paralysis of analysis* can occur when intellectual problem-solving processes are imposed over areas of life that may not be innately problematic. In its extreme, this refers to the overly analytical habit of creating problems where none exist just to have problems to obsess over. When this Mercury is neglected, we can lack critical thinking and/or nitpick over inconsequential points. Mercury frustration can be a symptom of a hungry intellect that needs to be fed by an intellectual task or organizational project to satiate its appetite for order. Feed the mind and the mind leaves you alone—until it's hungry, again.

6th HOUSE—STATE OF EMPLOYMENT
Skill Sets & Routines, Quality of Life, Health

The experiences of this state refer to the various rituals and routines to maintain and improve the quality of life we have grown accustomed to and/or that we strive to improve. This is where and how our *work ethic* develops which can also define the kinds of tools employed to get the job done. Planets residing here represent forces that are activated whenever we apply ourselves within any work environment or service-oriented labor. Sixth house experiences include immersion in personal and community businesses; the hustle of our time-as-money, punch-clock economic schedules; and training for skill sets and technologies necessary to meet the tasks at hand. Apprenticeships and trade schools can also be indicated here.

The 6th state governor can indicate the employment conditions best suited to our temperament and where we may benefit from apprenticeship with someone more skillful. There can be a strong bias for strong preparation and an industrious style for engineering the results.

Work-related stresses of the toil and drudgery of daily exertion take their toll on health. The 6th house symbolizes how we manage or mismanage our various stresses and survival anxieties. In medical astrology, each of the twelve signs link to a specific area of our anatomy. The 6th state governor can indicate the most stress-sensitive area of our body that acts up first when overworking reaches our maximum stress point. If we have the ears to hear, we can respond to the body's voice and stop overstressing before serious health problems take hold.

ANATOMY OF THE 12 SIGNS (Styles)

Aries—head, face, brain, the eyes
Taurus—throat, neck, shoulders, thyroid gland, vocal tract
Gemini—arms, lungs, hands, nervous system
Cancer—chest, breasts, stomach, alimentary canal
Leo—heart, chest, spine, spinal column, upper back
Virgo—digestive system, intestines, spleen, nervous system
Libra—kidneys, skin, lumbar region, buttocks
Scorpio—reproductive system, bowels, excretory system
Sagittarius—hips, thighs, liver, sciatic nerve
Capricorn—knees, joints, skeletal system
Aquarius—ankles, calves, circulatory system
Pisces—feet, lymphatic system, adipose tissue

Balance Point (12th House)

When the mounting pressures and stresses of employment overwhelm or begin to diminish health, balance can be discovered through 12th house experiences of escape, vacations and/or spiritual practices to decompress. When excessive 6th house experiences exhaust us with overdoing, we can find relief by "undoing ourselves" through retreating far away from the busy, noisy work force of the village.

Libra, Venus, 7th House
(State of Intimacy), the Descendent

LIBRA; Cardinal Air (A Pendulum)

As a Marriage archetype, the Cardinal Air style symbolizes relationship contracts bridging the self and the other. These contracts are made up of agreements between individuals that help equalize the nature of their interactions. Libra loves equality and harmonizes the contraries within human nature by oscillating between opposites to find balance. Its totem, THE SCALES OF JUSTICE, represents this process of mediation between opposing situations and viewpoints to find middle ground. Ambivalence arises when Libra is caught between opposing positions and unable or unwilling to take sides. Libra represents *grace in motion,* navigating situations that seem to happen by themselves, without decisions or exertions of will. Contrary to the docile stereotype, Libra is a style of extremes—like an acrobat walking a tightrope between opposing poles, across any spectrum of experience from one end to the other and back again.

LIBRA Shadow: ambivalence, indecision, passive-aggressive

The LIBRA Governor, or House Cusp

Whatever House Libra governs symbolizes an area where equality, harmony and fairness may need to be present before fully experiencing that state. It can also indicate where partnership may do well and working in tandem with another to navigate that state's experience. The state Libra governs can provide clues to qualities we may find attractive in our mates and marriages and also the conditions that can support longevity in relationship. Libra governs any state where equality matters more than hierarchy.

Libra Cusp Examples

3: communication occurs best between equals
6: joint business ventures, marriages serving a business
9: an egalitarian worldview, an all-inclusive philosophy
11: friendship as a basis for partnership and marriage

VENUS, a Graceful Force of Beauty

The graceful Libra spirit of Venus represents a longing for intimacy and the promise of courtship. This Venus carries a refined aesthetic appreciation for beauty in all artistic expressions and fashion. This Venusian quality of *allure* is written into our DNA to assure species survival. Almost all animals, plants and insects display visual, kinesthetic and olfactory behavior integral to pollination, mating, conception and procreation. The effortless and mysterious quality of *grace* reveals a more subtle force of beauty through elegance and refinement.

Aspect Notes

When Venus shares aspects with the transpersonal forces of Uranus, Neptune or Pluto, a resonance may be felt for a kind of love beyond personal love and beyond the mundane, for grand romance of the "one great love." The archetype of the Dream Lover, the Anima or Animus, may be guiding the inner psychic life. When Venus aspects other personal forces, the sense of value and aesthetics are usually shaped and influenced by them. Venus beautifies.

The Shadow of Venus (Libra Aspect)

When over-emphasized, the Libra side of Venus can act out in passive-aggressive behavior to avoid confrontation, crisis or conflict. The usually fair-minded Libra-style Venus can also turn increasingly indecisive from excessive *fence-sitting*, not knowing when or how to take a stand when necessary. When beauty becomes the main or only criteria for defining value, the ego personality can become increasingly one-sided or shallow. Negative judgments can be projected onto anyone or anything failing to measure up to one's exalted aesthetic standards.

The neglected Venus (of the Libra aspect) can indicate a lack of personal taste or interest in knowing what to like and not like. It can also act out as qualities that may be seen as repulsive and also as a disinterest in appearing attractive to others. In its extreme absence, there can be a hatred or total disinterest in Art of any kind.

THE DESCENDENT (7th House Cusp)

This symbol opposes the Ascendant and represents the qualities we tend to be attracted to in potential mates. These qualities already exist in our own subconscious and are projected onto those who personify them until they can be embraced within ourselves. The Descendent can symbolize a series of conditions—a kind of checklist of qualities—that help us stay related with a mate *as long as they can be maintained.* If these "boxes" become unchecked, the relationship can destabilize. The sign on the Descendent is also the governor of the 7th State of Intimacy and can indicate what we can share with another and also, the type of individuals that become attracted to us.

State of Intimacy Checklist

Aries: takes charge, confidence, bold, exciting, direct
Taurus: physical attraction, loyalty, trust, simplifies one's life
Gemini: good communication, youthful, covers the details
Cancer: nurturing, family-oriented, sensitive, artistic
Leo: charismatic, entertaining, playful, creative, adventurous

7th HOUSE—STATE OF INTIMACY
What We Attract and What Is Shared

The transition from 6th to 7th houses bridges the lower and upper hemispheres of the entire chart. With the lower six houses representing stages of self-development, the upper six houses link the developing self to greater realities starting with the 7th house of interpersonal relations, the State of Intimacy. Natal 7th house planets can indicate something of what we have to offer another in partnership and marriage. 7th house planets symbolize forces that become active whenever we engage in any one-to-one relationship, whether that be intimate, business partners, friendships, marriage or with an enemy.

7th house experience includes courtship, an offering of self, and shared vulnerability (sex is more 8th house than 7th). Since much of what passes for "relationships" can be tainted or distorted by unwanted psychological projections, interpersonal relations can be one of the more challenging experiences to many. Planets transiting through the 7th house can coincide with new experiences of love and intimacy in existing relationships and, if single, the arrival of new potential partners.

Balance Point (1st House)

When we become overly-identified as "a couple" or suffer loss of individual integrity by overextending ourselves in the life of another person, we can restore our sense of selfhood by embodying our Rising Sign (The Ascendant) and engaging 1st house experiences of self-discovery to reclaim our personal energy, interests and boundaries.

Scorpio, Pluto, Mars, 8th House
(State of Surrender)

Experiential Astrology

SCORPIO; Fixed Water (A Glacier)

A Changeling archetype, Scorpio is the only astrological archetype identified by multiple totems—*spider, scorpion, serpent, vulture, eagle, dove, Phoenix*—symbolizing its metamorphic nature for constantly outgrowing previous forms of itself. Its namesake totem, the SCORPION, is a vulnerable arachnid that finds refuge under rocks and inside hollow dead trees until it comes out to hunt. Privacy, secrecy and stealth are Scorpio strategies for protecting its sensitive inner core. Scorpions can survive in the blazing desert, showing a toughness for enduring adversity; hard exterior, soft interior. Scorpio's stinger is its defense to any threat which it uses to penetrate and extract the essence from whatever situation or obstacle it faces. Fixed Water symbolizes the *passions* of concentrated feeling that guides Scorpio's inner life and defines its amoral compass.

SCORPIO Shadow: possessive, compulsive, anti-social

The SCORPIO Governor, or House Cusp

Scorpio governs the state where passion and strong feelings guide and define the experience. There can be a thirst for intensity, change, and even crisis. Depending on the forces in this state, this area can be subject to obsession and compulsive behavior as an orientation for navigating experience with intense focus. This state can also favor secrecy and a strategic and stealthy approach to situations.

Scorpio Cusp Examples

3: learns best when subject arouses passion
5: intensity of feeling stirs creativity
9: an investigative approach to philosophy
11: a few close friends, many acquaintances

MARS (Also in this Set)

The force of Mars—*as part of the Scorpio, Pluto and 8th House set*—refers chiefly to the visceral force of sexual arousal and response, and the sexual sport of chasing and being chased. This martial force bypasses morality (unless aspecting Jupiter or Saturn) by objectifying sex, thrilling at being the object of desire, and/or pursuing the object of desire. In the sporting game of sex, territorial possessiveness can arise if inflamed desires are projected onto another. If Mars refers to the physical sex act between adults, Pluto refers to the deeper invisible processes of conception, birth and death.

PLUTO, a Regenerative Force of Transformation

Pluto, along with the other two transpersonal forces of Uranus and Neptune, represents where and how our personal lives interface with greater impersonal realities of sociopolitical, historical, and collective shifts that define an era. These transpersonal forces can also act as Muses that can guide, distract, destroy and inspire us. With the Muse spirit of Pluto, the spiritual meets the personal and the personal becomes political.

"Spiritual" here refers to what astrologer Jeffrey Wolf Green calls *the soul intent*. Between incarnations, the disincarnate soul drifts through the bardo and reincarnates into its next life with *a voracious appetite* for a specific human experience needed to evolve. The essences that feed the hungry soul nurture its embodiment into the human condition. These essences are defined by the experiences in natal Pluto's house placement. Examples:

Plutonic Hunger for Soulful Experience

1st House Pluto: a hunger for self-discovery and novelty
2nd House Pluto: a hunger for proving one's survival
3rd House Pluto: a hunger for endless learning
4th House Pluto: a hunger for belonging

Experiential Astrology

The transpersonal force of Pluto represents a wild spectrum of experiences with the powers of regeneration, degeneration and many forms of death and rebirth. As the Plutonic experiences (its house) are engaged, a transforming regenerative force increases and can be felt as a certain kind of *empowerment* (defined by Pluto's house placement). When these experiences are neglected or disengaged, Pluto's transformative force can *reverse* into a degenerative influence which can be experienced as power loss, feelings of helplessness, and misguided obsessions. *Feed the soul and regenerate your energy; starve the soul and suffer degeneration.*

Trauma, Obsession and Healing

Pluto's natal placement can indicate the area of our lives where we may be prone to obsession and obsessive behaviors. Not all obsessions are equal; some are creative, some are destructive. Obsession in and of itself points to where tremendous energy is focused in direct intuitive engagement with the life force. Obsession can also indicate a stage in the healing of *unprocessed trauma*. During and after traumatic experiences, the ego lives through a shock of destabilization. In response to this shock, the ego attempts to re-stabilize through fixation or obsession on something or someone. This can be work, drugs, sex, lovers, money, whatever. Unfortunately, not every obsession is healthy or productive. Many obsessions are misguided and do not, and cannot, heal trauma.

Pluto's natal placement pinpoints the specific obsession capable of supporting the healing process by rejuvenating the life force within the individual. Plutonic obsession creates an internal fire that burns *the dross of personal reactivity* to the shock that keeps the ego attached to the trauma. Once this reactivity is burned out, the initial trauma is drained of the emotional charge that kept the ego in a repeating pattern of redundancy to buffer itself from the shock.

Only plutonic obsession can ignite the internal fire to drain the emotion from the trauma. Though other obsessions can temporarily alleviate the suffering of trauma, at best they can only act as buffers and at worst, self-destruction and suicide. Through plutonic obsession, the ego can undergo its own process of death and rebirth towards self-reinvention. Pluto the Healer.

Plutonic Obsession

5th House Pluto: immersion in creative process and art
6th House Pluto: meaningful work and service to others
9th House Pluto: vision quests and philosophical study
10th House Pluto: joining a transpersonal cause
12th House Pluto: meditation retreats

When the Personal Becomes the Political

Activation of natal Pluto arouses a specific kind of power as *a potent force of influence*. Whenever the experience of Pluto's house is engaged, Pluto activates and eventually *politicizes the person* by virtue of that specific experience of power. Being "politicized" by Pluto has little or nothing to do with any political party—the Left, Right, Centrist, Libertarian or Arch-Conservative. Activation of natal Pluto turns us into political pundits of a certain influence, depending on its house placement and, also, by any aspects Pluto shares with other planets. Pluto is where the spiritual meets the personal and the personal becomes political. What kind of power can you get behind? Look to natal Pluto.

In Pluto's world, there are at least twelve ways to define and know power. As Pluto gains traction by its activation, a distinct political influence comes through the person who has discovered how to feed their hungry soul. What constitutes *the political* becomes revisioned through how this natal plutonic influence impacts the world around us, regardless of party affiliations, by personal alignment with the inner power sources symbolized by natal Pluto. *Not my will but Thy will be done on earth as in heaven. Become the change you want to see in the world.*

The Shadow of Pluto

When drawn into a downward degenerative cycle—by neglecting to feed the soul (as described)—compensatory behavior can erupt in an attempt to replace power with control. However, power is not the same as control. Trying to control *what or who cannot be controlled* can be an obsessive attempt to avoid feelings of powerlessness. This type of obsession for control dramatizes one part of Pluto's shadow aspect.

At the other extreme, when Pluto is over-emphasized, empowerment obsessions can force the person into psychic burnout and spiritual exhaustion. If the empowered person cannot or will not channel the plutonic force through a transpersonal cause or mission, it can implode in the body. Plutonic shadow work starts with knowing where you are with power and aligning yourself with the kind of power you can live with. These assessments require knowledge and understanding of Pluto's house placement and the experiences symbolized there.

Plutonic Empowerment

6th House Pluto: the power of service to great causes
7th House Pluto: the power of a great life-changing love
8th House Pluto: the power to catalyze meaningful change
9th House Pluto: the power of vision and perspective
10th House Pluto: the power of far-reaching influence
11th House Pluto: the power of the community catalyst

Aspect Notes

When Pluto shares aspects with personal forces, they undergo lifelong *transformations* by outgrowing or molting obsolete versions of themselves. Venus outgrows old ways of loving, Mars outgrows stagnating motivations, Mercury outgrows obsolete thinking styles, etc. Pluto transforms.

8th HOUSE—STATE OF SURRENDER

What Evolves Us Makes Us Resilient

Traditionally, the 8th house refers to sex, death, taxes, other people's money and values, inheritances, larger governing bodies (such as governments and corporations), and "acts of god" (such as weather catastrophes, earthquakes and volcanic eruptions). All of these events refer to experiences beyond our personal control and often beyond personal comprehension. The State of Surrender offers immersive and chaotic experiences as *evolutionary triggers* that challenge ego-flexibility and the resiliency for facing real life shocks, losses and the endings of life cycles. The State of Surrender can also be ecstatic when powerful sexual orgasms shock ego-control into spasms of somatic rapture. Certain rituals, meditations and psychoactive drug experiences can also trigger powerful transformative experiences that evolve us.

8th House Cusp

The sign governing the 8th house, the State of Surrender, can indicate the characteristics of a person's sexual style and arousal criteria for how they're turned on. For more details, include the planet (force) associated with the cusp sign for additional sexy details, i.e., a Gemini 8th house cusp and Mercury, Aries 8th house cusp and Mars.

At essence, the 8th house refers to experiences of *meaningful change*; not every change is meaningful. What makes any transformation meaningful depends on whether or not it results in a more meaningful existence as opposed to merely producing a shift of mood or a concept of transformation but no lasting change. The 8th state governor can indicate what constitutes meaningful change and this differs for each person.

By engaging the attributes and characteristics of the 8th state governor, we can temporarily relax identification with the Rising Sign and enter the State of Surrender. An otherwise flighty Gemini Rising person might find meaningful change when accepting a position of authority by embodying their 8th State Capricorn governor. Leo Rising individuals with Pisces at the 8th house cusp might discover meaningful change beyond their usually self-confident persona in a deepening receptivity and empathy for others.

The 8th house can be a bit like the junkyard of the chart, given the swirl of chaos and the multiple levels of unconscious instinctual realities represented there. As Scorpio and Pluto symbolize both reproductive and elimination systems, sexually transmitted diseases and repressed emotional sewage are represented here as well as the high spiritual yogas of tantra and kundalini. At essence, experiences in the State of Surrender incite ego-death and rebirth, a process of dying to one version of oneself and midwifing a more pared down essential version of ourselves, wizened by and to the ways of change.

Sadly, not every ego-death results in rebirth. If any ego-death is mistaken for actual physical death, suicidal ideations and follow-through can occur. This can happen if there's over-identification with a self-image and a fierce resistance to releasing attachment to that ego *as it disintegrates*. If ego-identification can be relaxed and released, the old ego can die off in a similar way a serpent molts an old skin so it can grow larger. This kind of "ego molting" into ego rebirth can take anywhere from a few days to a few years depending on how complete the state of surrender is. There's also the faith and patience required during the interim between who we have been and who we are becoming. Every rebirth has its own timing and cannot be forced.

Balance Point (2nd House)

When over-saturated with too much personal growth and trauma, balance can be found in 2nd house experiences of whatever provides a sense of consistency and lasting value to our lives. Sometimes this can be as simple as tending to daily chores, meeting survival agendas, or clarifying security priorities. The 2nd house points to how we stabilize or "normalize" ourselves during crisis, shocks, and traumas. How to alleviate the existential angst of going through more changes than we know how to process and assimilate? Return to your core values.

Sagittarius, Jupiter, 9th House
(State of Faith)

SAGITTARIUS; Mutable Fire (A Shooting Star)

A Voyager archetype, Sagittarius represents a swiftness of momentum in an open-ended direction that doesn't need to know where it's going so long as *it's going somewhere*. Through expanding consciousness, Sagittarius sees the Big Picture, asks the Big Questions, and knows the Big Answers—*or believes it does*. Sagittarius' mythical half-man/half-horse CENTAUR totem symbolizes a cohesion of animal instinct and human spirit. The Centaur's lust for life animates its restless feral spirit, and stimulates the human attribute for abstraction to view the world as if from afar. Sagittarius' gambling spirit takes risks to increase opportunities and mobility. Mutable Fire circulates intuition in all directions at once allowing for a more direct experience of *the energy* in any given situation, thing or person *while in motion*.

SAGITTARIUS Shadow: *flashy, opportunistic, dogmatic*

The SAGITTARIUS Governor, or House Cusp

Whatever state Sagittarius governs refers to an area where we can take more risks to expand opportunities. Experiences in this state may be inclined to a sense of adventure, where the thrill of taking flight and leaps of faith push us past familiar limitations. The Sagittarius governor can also indicate a need for believing in the experience of that state, that it has a future, before fully appreciating the experience.

Sagittarius Cusp Examples

1: an expansive persona or personal style
3: intuitive learning style that can teach what it learns
7: attracted to adventurous mates (from other cultures?)
10: unity of personal vision and public image

JUPITER, an Expansive Force of Perspective

In Vedic Sidereal astrology Jupiter is known as "the guru" planet. The teacher spirit of Jupiter works through the context of *higher learning,* a phrase that traditionally means university level education. However, the context of higher learning can be relative and known in far more personal ways based on natal Jupiter's sign and house placement. I like to think that higher learning begins with an awareness of ignorance and where a certain blindness or naiveté exists.

Jupiter's house placement can indicate *a lack of conscience* in a specific area that acts out as recklessness, bombast or simple naiveté. Depending on other factors, this ignorance can remain unconscious up to the third Jupiter return at 36 years; exceptions include quick learners and those given to engaging consciousness-expanding experiments. Jupiter's natal placement can sometimes indicate where those experiences, symbolized by its natal house position, were sorely neglected or betrayed in a past life. Past life karma can be indicated by the sign and house placement of the South Node. Natal Jupiter points to where we are seeking to *restore our faith* in an area where it may have been destroyed or diminished in a past life.

Higher learning, as redefined here, refers to whatever experiences are necessary to expand consciousness in a previous area of ignorance, an area that may also lack in conscientiousness. Someone with Jupiter in Pisces or the 12th House might know higher learning as empathy and a felt sense of unity with all of life. Those with Jupiter in Leo or the 5th house may discover higher learning through a discovery of joy, creative play, and art. Those with Jupiter in Aquarius or the 11th house might know higher learning as the development of social conscience.

A one-word description of the Jupiter influence might be "more." When the force of Jupiter is activated, consciousness expands in that area and more reality of that state is perceived. When the aperture of perception dilates, we perceive what actually matters and doesn't matter, and more of what is worth caring about and what isn't. This perceptual shift marks a transition from *expanding consciousness into conscience.*

Examples of Jupiter Conscience-Building

4th House: personal ethics set apart from family morality
6th House: conscientious work ethic and health care
10th House: the ethics around publicizing one's vision
12th House: faith in unknowns for a spiritual conscience

As conscience develops, an ethos and personal ethical code forms around the perception of what makes any situation or action good or bad, right or wrong. Ethos differs from morality. The former originates in personal observations and judgement calls, whereas the latter is more an expression of the codes of conduct inherited from family, church and public education systems.

Integration of Jupiter continues from the development of conscience into a personal ethos and whatever belief system and philosophy best represents *how we know truth*; not "THE" truth, but one's own truth. When this distinction is forgotten and our personal truth is confused for "the" universal truth, Jupiter's shadow aspect surfaces as *the fundamentalist virus (FV)*. Careful—a FV pandemic has spread across the land and this virus has been known to be highly contagious.

Aspect Notes

When Jupiter shares aspects with the transpersonal forces of Uranus, Neptune or Pluto, personal perception becomes tested against universal truths towards greater alignment with them. The archetype of the Teacher may be guiding the inner psychic life. When Jupiter aspects other personal forces, they can be amplified and sometimes exaggerated, as if to draw more attention to their purpose. Jupiter expands.

The Shadow of Jupiter

When Jupiter's natal placement becomes overemphasized, it can indicate where and how we've become prone to exaggeration and are making a bigger deal of ourselves or our experiences than necessary. There may be good karmic reason for making a big deal of Jupiter's placement, where exaggeration may be required to get our full attention. However, when the big Jupiter force is not tempered, it can distort into bombastic behavior, overblown assumptions, con jobs, and a misplaced sense of entitlement.

When Jupiter remains neglected and unintegrated, we can lose perspective and lose track of what we believe in and stand for. We might even assume that we have no beliefs or perhaps we parrot the beliefs and views of others whose views we exalt over our own. Whether it's over-emphasized or neglected or repressed, symptoms of Jupiter's shadow include tunnel vision and an absence of humor, especially about oneself. When our world starts appearing less funny and more claustrophobic, it may be a good time to check in with Jupiter.

9th HOUSE—STATE OF FAITH

Morality, Ethics, Beliefs, Religion, Philosophy

The three major world religions—*Christianity, Buddhism, Islam*—all originated from singular visionary epiphanies of one individual. Yet Jesus of Nazareth was not a Christian; Gautama Buddha, or Siddhartha, was not a Buddhist; and Muhammad was no convert to Islam. All three world religions developed over time as more individuals and groups became magnetized around the spiritual principles these rare individuals embodied as living truths. After years, decades, and centuries, their initial epiphanies were encoded into belief systems, dogmas, doctrines and holy books by various clergy in an attempt to keep the faith alive. This conversion from authentic spiritual revelations into religious dogmas and doctrines lies at the root of the State of Faith.

We humans are possessed of an uncanny talent for making a religion out of almost anything: football, sex, whiskey, rock'n'roll, celebrities, astrology, the internet, television—the list continues into eternity. The 9th house might just as well represent the "altar" of the chart with its planets (forces) symbolizing the holy icons of experience exalted above everything else. These forces become activated during any experience that expands consciousness beyond the 'reality tunnels' of daily mundane existence. Long distance travel, culture shock, universities, religion and philosophy, vision quests, and mind-expanding drugs are examples of how consciousness expands and tests our beliefs and assumptions about the world we live in.

Faith, in its purer sense, is not about religion or philosophy, nor is it a belief or a dogma, but an intuitive capacity for investing in unknowns. To take *a leap of faith* means to move forward without knowledge of the outcome. Preconceptions and expectations are replaced by intuition and an openness to possibility. These kinds of experiences can feel like standing on a mountaintop or seeing the world below from a bird's-eye view.

As consciousness continues expanding, perception can dilate to such extremes that words fail to convey the experience, alienating us from those who cannot understand or share our vision yet. The sign governing the 9th house can indicate a spiritual orientation of how we come to know truth and then, define our beliefs and the philosophy about it. When these beliefs turn into dogmas, we might try to convince or convert others to our way of seeing (refer to THE SHADOW OF JUPITER). *FV alert!*

Balance Point (3rd House)

When blinded by our own beliefs and assumptions, 3rd house experiences can restore balance by any exposure to *the relative nature of things,* of how all truths simply express one point of view. Relativity means any experience can be interpreted in a number of ways; what can appear deep and meaningful to one perspective can be seen as ridiculous to another. By developing 3rd house communication skills, 9th house alienation can be broken down as we find the symbols and language to share our big visions with others.

Capricorn, Saturn, 10th House (Professional State), the Midheaven

CAPRICORN; Cardinal Earth (A Monument)

A Leader archetype, the pragmatic style of Capricorn consolidates ambition and focus to achieve goals of personal and professional accomplishment. As a Cardinal Earth style, Capricorn represents intention methodically moving towards manifestation. Its totem, THE MOUNTAIN GOAT, follows a zigzag path up the cliffs to the mountain top, each step leading to the next ledge until the peak is reached. Capricorn's sober, self-organizing intelligence realizes its aims with caution and a scrutiny for distractions that might derail success. A fear of failure or making mistakes can sometimes overshadow ambition and frustrate advancement. Capricorn's vulnerability comes from an inclination to be on display, to be seen, and thus, become available to praise as well as persecution from others and the world.

CAPRICORN Shadow: cold, grim, tyrannical, ruthless

The CAPRICORN Governor, or House Cusp

Any state governed by Capricorn symbolizes an area where a bit more structure, respect and status (recognition) may be necessary. The experience in Capricorn's state may require a more methodical, well-organized and prepared approach. There can be a goal-oriented ambition here for using the experience of the state to advance oneself. This state can also arouse vulnerable feelings of hyper-sensitivity to public opinion, criticism and judgments from others.

Capricorn Cusp Examples

3: learning topics to teach or write about
4: a prestige and status defined family upbringing
7: attraction to mates who can advance one's ambitions
9: conservative religious or philosophical views
12: repressed needs for taking on authority and status

SATURN, A Compressive Force of Commitment

The Crone, or Senex, spirit of Saturn's natal placement represents a state where more structure, personal effort, and hard work may be needed to overcome fears of failure before any worthwhile success can be achieved. Natal Saturn can point to an area of *personal inadequacy* until it's faced and accepted as part of growing up. This maturation process starts with identifying the specific fears defined by Saturn's house placement and sign and then, over time, *converting these fears into commitments*, i.e., committing to the very thing you're afraid of. In esoteric astrology and Tarot, Saturn symbolizes The Devil archetype. The boogeyman is only truly scary to the Child Within, not the Mature Adult.

As an 11th house Saturn person, the Devil was always other people to me, especially the fear of crowds; the herd! I've been afraid of herd mentality since childhood, starting with schoolyard social insecurity. It wasn't until I began converting my *fear of people* into an ongoing commitment to people—through structuring the group dynamics for creating theatre and cinema—that I began experiencing Saturn's hidden power for increasing the capacity to *manifest my intentions*. The deeper I committed to groups in my own way, the more I started manifesting my dreams and ambitions—not just within 11th house group experiences, but across the board; everywhere. *Saturn magick!*

Natal Saturn can also symbolize high standards, whether we are aware of them or not, and where self-doubt increases when those standards are not met. Saturnine self-work continues by identifying the nature of these high standards and mustering the commitment to raise the bar to meet those standards ourselves. If we do not, we suffer *the double standard* of expecting from others what we cannot yet deliver.

Examples of Saturn Fears

1st House: fear of existing or not existing
2nd House: fear that there's no security in the world
4th House: fear of not belonging anywhere

7th House: fear of intimacy and of losing oneself
9th House: fear that there's nothing to believe in

Saturn can also symbolize the nature of our *true responsibility* beyond the impersonal, socially-accepted codes of what it means to be "a responsible adult or citizen." Many become responsible on society's terms yet can fail as persons. This can become clear whenever we're faced with a pressing need to achieve more *success and status*. Whether conforming to impersonal cultural definitions of *success and status* or those defined by oneself, the results determine the kind of success we will live with. Some actually do better conforming to external standards, while others do better living on their own terms. Saturn becomes integrated either way, as we learn how to manage the time of our lives and manifest our dreams and ambitions in the real world.

Aspect Notes

When Saturn shares aspects with the transpersonal forces of Uranus, Neptune or Pluto, there can be an attempt to give form and structure to their expression in time and space. The archetype of the Senex may be guiding the inner psychic life. When Saturn aspects other personal forces, there can be an accentuated sense of limitations and inadequacies in this area. As natal Saturn becomes integrated, through becoming more accountable for our fears and shortcomings, these forces can tend to undergo their own maturation processes. Saturn consolidates.

The Shadow of Saturn

An over-emphasized Saturn can distort through rigid, overly-structured parameters imposed on life experience resulting in too many rules, regulations and conditions. A *calcification* can occur, a kind of spiritual arthritis, inhibiting spontaneity and creativity where duty, work and sober responsibility have become overly dominant. We may take ourselves too seriously or act out assumed superiority through obnoxious authoritative behavior. In its extreme, we might bear the sorrowful burden of over-manifestation and its jaded loss of joy from in the absence of new possibilities and potentials.

An unintegrated or repressed Saturn can manifest as avoidance, fear or dread of authority, whether of one's own authority or authority figures like police, bosses, teachers, parents, doctors, etc. An unconscious Saturn can also appear as *incompetence* in the house it resides in and/or a reluctance to fully commit to anything, in or out of that house. *Commitment phobia.* Those with a neglected Saturn may unconsciously seek approval from others they project saturnine qualities onto—*competence, expertise, integrity*—while secretly resenting themselves and/or the external authority figures for their own *feelings of inadequacy.*

Those with an unintegrated Saturn tend to be "reality-challenged" around time management (late for appointments?) and integrity loss (lacking follow through, having trouble "keeping word"?), drifting through life without an anchor. An integrated Saturn works like an anchor and a rudder for those sailing into the manifest world of time, space and knowledge.

The MIDHEAVEN (10th House Cusp)

Whatever sign rules the 10th house (aka the Midheaven, or MC) represents our *public style,* or how we may appear to the public. The MC of our Public Image can indicate the first impression the impersonal public has about us. Much of public opinion rests on confidence, or lack of, in what we propose or promise to deliver. The Midheaven sign symbolizes something about what we have to offer the world.

The idea is that public credibility can be increased or decreased depending on the extent the attributes of that sign are delivered—or not. For example, with Virgo at my MC, I've somehow maintained public credibility in a *spirit of service by offering methods and skills.* I discovered this years ago after displaying too much Scorpio intensity in public and failing miserably. Those with more conservative styles at the MC—*like Taurus, Capricorn, Saturn, Pisces*—might build public credibility by not deviating from the *status quo.*

Others with more radical Midheaven signatures—*like Uranus, Mars, Sagittarius, Aquarius*—might gain public confidence with more unconventional presentations and products. The Midheaven sign represents "the goods" you have to offer. Deliver the goods and you're rewarded with the credibility of public confidence in your offering.

10th HOUSE—PROFESSIONAL STATE
"What Do I Want to Be When I Grow Up?"

At essence, 10th house experience starts with the question, "What Do I Want to Be When I Grow Up?", a fantasy born in the childhood imagination for playing a special role on the world stage. The Professional State indicates where personal ambitions find expression through a career, and how we can build a niche to stand out amidst the fierce competition of the public marketplace. Professionals become invested in protecting the integrity and credibility of their *reputation*. However, due to fickle public opinion, reputation cannot truly be controlled. Public image can be fragile and easily damaged or destroyed by slander or scandal. When our services and products are on display to the impersonal public at large, we can naturally feel overly-sensitive to scrutiny, criticism and outright attack.

10th house planets symbolize forces that can energize our Professional State after our goals have been clearly defined and are in the process of being achieved. When activated, these forces project out into the public, shaping how we are represented and impacting those we call clients, customers and consumers. When transiting planets enter the Professional State, we can experience more public exposure, promotions and a sense of advancement. How this may appear to you and others depends on the particular transiting planets.

When Jupiter passes through the 10th house every twelve years, there may be a kind of spotlight effect highlighting your career. If Saturn passes through here, you may find yourself in a harvest cycle of working harder than ever to get all those apples to market before they rot. With any of the three transpersonal forces transiting the 10th house, you may start noticing your personal and professional life overlapping the greater sociopolitical and economic shifts and trends of the day.

Balance Point (4th House)

When our professional ambitions dominate our lives, we can sometimes lose touch with the underlying support systems and people who helped us succeed. Without the sustaining power of 4th house down-time, self-nourishment and emotional support, we can also suffer public over-exposure, burnout, or worse yet, sell out, lose our soul, and turn hard and cold on the inside.

Aquarius, Uranus, 11th House
(Community State)

AQUARIUS; Fixed Air (A Lightning Storm)

A Tribal archetype, the Fixed Air style of Aquarius *concentrates the mind* within the highly interactive collective dimension of socialization. Eccentric Aquarius subverts the *status quo* to revision what it means to be human. Aquarius represents the impersonal We, the voice of Humanity, on a mission to liberate itself and others from tyranny, oppression and conformity. The Aquarius style has this peculiar capacity for detachment in its ability to disconnect from groupthink to experiment with new ways of thinking and inventing new models of social discourse. A spectrum-like quality infuses humanitarian Aquarius with a wide array of angles to explore multiple points of view.

AQUARIUS Shadow: elitist, disingenuous, aloof

The AQUARIUS Governor, or House Cusp

Experiences in the states governed by Aquarius can indicate areas demanding mental concentration. These states can also thrive in community participation, the formation of new social bonds, and friendships. A certain detachment here can indicate a lack of emotional investment, affording more freedom to come and go. There can be an inclination to experiment and tinker. The Aquarius governor can bring more objectivity, political interests, social activism, and a wider range of interests.

Aquarius Cusp Examples

1: tribal-identified, friend to all, multifaceted personality
3: decoding group minds, giving voice to the collective
9: nontraditional religious or philosophical views
10: professional activism, humanitarian ambitions

URANUS, a Liberating Force of Awakening

Uranus resides in the State where specific patterns of oppression may continue to shroud our *innate autonomy* until we're awakened to it. Uranus does not refer to the freedom of "do anything you want at any time or buy anything you want because you have money"; that's instant gratification consumer trance. True freedom expresses an innate state obscured by oppression. Remove or bypass the oppression and freedom reigns. Over decades of societal, media, teacher/parent, and peer conditioning, the collective has lapsed into a complex cultural trance of various types of oppression. Natal Uranus points to a specific type of oppression enslaving each of us since childhood.

The awakening of natal Uranus can sometimes occur as a freedom *from* something. Examples: 9th house Uranus can indicate early religious programming. Once exposed as a source of oppression, freedom *from* religion can allow for the discovery of spirituality without dogma. 4th house Uranus can symbolize parental programs instilling guilt and punishment for simply being a naive child. Once exposed as a source of oppression, freedom *from* family morality can liberate a life lived by one's own code. Those with 2nd house Uranus may be oppressed by societal values around money and security that, once exposed, can result in freedom *from* the 9 to 5 punch-clock economic slavery of work by earning income in a manner that does not compromise our autonomy.

The house placement of natal Uranus can indicate a startling stubbornness for *zero compromise*. When waking up to our true freedom, it may be impossible to return to the old ways. This *waking up* may come as a revealing more than any kind of willed achievement. As we grow more secure in our true freedom, autonomy can no longer be threatened. As Uranus represents a transpersonal force that links the personal with the collective, we are also only as autonomous as the autonomy we can allow others. Knowing as much, some turn to social activism in a political revolution to awaken those around them, while others may walk a quieter path of living free by example.

Natal Uranus can also symbolize an area where we may require little to no structure or imposed limitations or parameters or conditions or how the experience of that state is navigated. It's where a certain brilliance and even genius can be tapped, given our willingness to go about the experience of that state completely in our own way; the "zero compromise" clause, again. As a result, the state Uranus inhabits can also be prone to a reflex of rebellion when we're encumbered by, or faced with, externally-imposed rules or how to manage the experience.

Aspect Notes

When Uranus shares aspects with personal forces, they undergo an *acceleration* of their innate processes—they speed up. Venus awakens to novel kinds of love, Mars acts quicker, Mercury processes information faster, etc. Uranus accelerates.

The Shadow of Uranus

An over-emphasized Uranus distorts when we become too independent for our own good, especially when our cherished freedom inhibits intimacy and bonding with others, or spins us out into a life of crime with no respect for the law or of citizens' rights. A neglected Uranus can act out in knee-jerk rebelliousness against anything or anybody threatening *bogus autonomy*. The *ego independence* of bogus autonomy can be easily confused for true freedom until exposed as the misguided sense of entitlement for always expecting to get your own way.

11th HOUSE—COMMUNITY STATE

Friends & Acquaintances Sharing Common Unity

We are identified as social creatures by how we define friendship and the kinds of groups we are drawn to—we are known by the company we keep. Groups we are repulsed by can also define us politically and socially. Friendships and the groups we join are time-tested to endure the greater sociopolitical shifts of each passing era. Community State planets (forces) can characterize *who we are in the village:* Mars the Doer, Jupiter the Teacher, Neptune the Dreamer. The social fabric of our lives weaves our personal lives into overlapping social circles—*from strangers to acquaintances to fans to actual friendships to local tribes and groups to larger societies.* The functions of 11th house planets indicate how we might attempt to become part of something greater than ourselves alone.

The Community State governor (house cusp) can indicate the qualities we may seek in friendships as well as something about our *social style* within groups—whether we're more passive (Pisces or Taurus) or more active (Aries or Gemini) or co-managing (Capricorn or Libra). How friendships are made and broken remains an essential 11th house criteria. *Friend or foe?* We know our friends by the pacts that bind us and our foes by the betrayals that separate us. This state can refer to how we approach and/or avoid the processes of community-building; how we fit into, or don't fit into, the social codes of how any group defines itself. 11th house experience points to tribal identity, social affiliations, group minds, and groupthink.

Balance Point (5th House)

When overwhelmed by the cacophony of too many voices, too many friends, and too much groupthink, we can find balance in 5th house creative states to discover and celebrate our own voice, our own story, our own world.

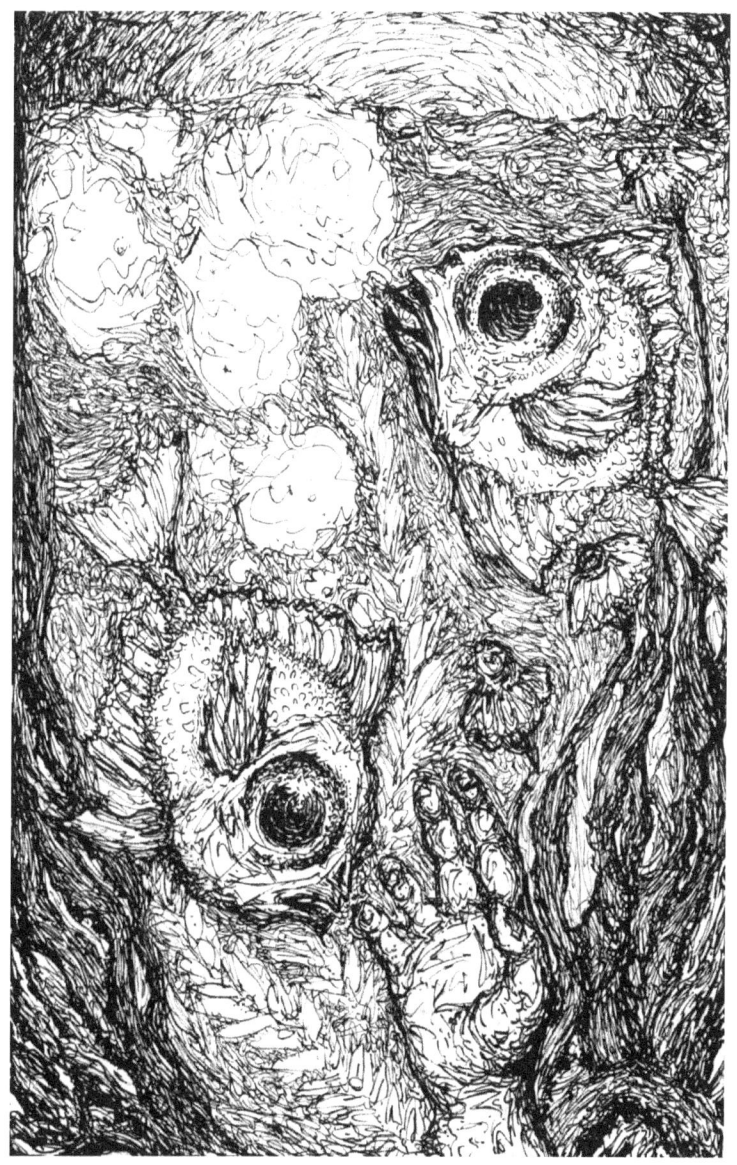

Pisces, Neptune, 12th House
(State of the Soul)

PISCES; Mutable Water (A Whirlpool)

A Siren Mermaid archetype, the fluid Mutable Water style of Pisces follows a path of least resistance to blend, dissolve and unify. The Pisces totem of TWO FISH swim in opposing directions, symbolizing contrary currents of emotion, moving between merging and withdrawing. Pisces represents the most receptive style of the Zodiac, capable of deep absorption of life energies. When Pisces reaches its saturation point and can absorb no longer, it naturally shuts down and disappears like fish escaping into subterranean caves. Pisces refers to the pure awareness of oceanic consciousness flowing everywhere at once, over boundaries and barriers, to envelop and to love. As the last sign of the zodiac, Pisces also represents endings of great cycles.

PISCES Shadow: self-pity, escapism, apathy, withdrawn

The PISCES Governor, or House Cusp

Whatever state Pisces governs symbolizes an area where a more receptive approach allows us to blend and merge with the experience and maybe even disappear into it. The Pisces state can also point to experiences where sensitive feelings require protection and empathy. This area can also render us vulnerable to victimization, either by ourselves or by others, due to a lack of defensive strategies beyond trying to escape or avoid any situation perceived as an immediate threat.

Pisces Cusp Examples

3: quiet, intuitive, poetic learning and thinking styles
4: passive domestic style, home as sanctuary or temple
7: attracted to qualities in another not easily analyzed
9: an "all is one" spiritual orientation

NEPTUNE, a Dreaming Force of Compassion

Like the steady crashing of waves turning rocky seashores into stones into pebbles into sand, Neptune (aka Poseidon), God of the

Seas, symbolizes the gradual erosion of arbitrary boundaries, borders and barriers. Neptune represents the shock of non-dual consciousness in the fertile void of *indivisibility*. Natal Neptune points to the invisible, pervasive power of our *greatest dreams and the sacrifices to be made* for bringing them into manifestation. Between our hidden expectations and lifelong aspirations and our greatest disappointments and delusions, Neptune's placement charts a lifelong path of disillusionment, suffering and enlightenment; *disillusionment is framed here as Neptunian enlightenment.*

The Ego Ideal and Soul-Identification

When unrealistic expectations are exposed as the illusions they can be, disillusionment sets in. As more illusions are dispelled, a clarity of vision emerges for seeing life more as it is, not how we think it should be. With the suffering of disappointment, more compassion is needed to endure the inner confrontations between the Ego ideal—*how we idealize ourselves and our lives*—and the deeper dimensions of the soul.

The Ego Ideal represents a primitive stage of Neptune in its boundless imagination for dreaming the impossible. Paradoxically, or not, it's the Ego Ideal that may need sacrificing before our greatest dreams can come true. Neptune points to an innate idealism and naïveté of real-life limitations within its state. Neptune's ongoing process of *disillusionment as enlightenment* illuminates the actual as the ideal, marking a spiritual shift from ego-identification to soul-identification. Only after the ego has been consistently defeated by the experience of the soul, can we align ourselves more fully with the essential.

Neptune and Sacrifice

Besides our expectations and disappointments, the placement of natal Neptune can also indicate where *our greatest sacrifices can occur*, and also where we have a certain capacity for sacrifice. What is meant by sacrifice here is the act of giving up something or someone very near and dear to our hearts; anything less cannot truly be called a *sacrifice*. Such sacrifices can occur when we are called to become part of a greater cause than our self-interest or personal survival. 11th house Neptune can sacrifice a social life for a cause; 1st house Neptune can sacrifice ego for a cause; 4th house Neptune can sacrifice family life for a cause.

When activated by sacrifices, Neptune can unleash a tsunami of psychic energy that inspires major life changes, identity reevaluations, and/or a dissolution of everything we have come to know as "reality". This can include a sense of disappearance where the usual sense of self can drift in and out of focus or vanish altogether. *Where do we go when we disappear?*

To sacrifice means to make sacred. When we put ego aside and allow Neptune's dreaming force to pass through us—*unobstructed by personal beliefs, preconceptions and theories*—a spiritual healing takes place. We may feel a new respect for the mystery at the heart of existence or a dissolution of defenses no longer required. Neptune's awesome force of dreaming cannot be reasoned with or figured out, though it can be experienced. We can be moved, inspired, transported by its waves and currents, but no maps exist to accurately define or predict its shifting weather patterns. Experiencing the Neptune energies can open a portal of intimacy with the void of pure potential where we are nothing, and it's not a problem.

Neptune, Escapism and God

Those with strongly placed Neptunes (especially in close aspect with Moon, Ascendant, Mercury, Venus or Sun) can exhibit stronger escapist tendencies and be more vulnerable to drug and/or alcohol addiction which offer a temporary escape from the physical body and material world pressures. At essence, Neptune points to the deep and often buried yearning for communion with God, Source and divinity to fulfill spiritual needs. Getting drunk and high can produce a subjective experience of a kind of communion with the spirit world; "spirits", another word for booze. Spiritual experience can obviously occur without drugs or booze through psycho-spiritual disciplines like yoga, meditation, dreamwork and various ritual processes such as Paratheatre.

When activated, the transpersonal force of Neptune can trigger a direct intuitive experience of the *dreambody* while fully awake as the electromagnetic field of our aura. When the Neptune current is turned on, we may identify with the *light body* of this aura more than our physical body. In its extreme, Neptune can link to *out of body experiences*. Natal Neptune can indicate where we naturally ignore boundaries and borders as if they don't exist or feel unnecessary.

Like Uranus and Pluto, Neptune cannot really be integrated as a conscious act. It is more like the ego becomes integrated by Neptune; *we become Neptunized as we're exposed to non-dual experiences.* Developing a supple imagination and staying close to our true sources of inspiration (music, poetry, cinema as Neptunian mediums) can enliven a more harmonious relationship with mysterious transpersonal Neptune.

Aspect Notes

When Neptune shares aspects with personal forces, they undergo softening and boundary dissolution towards a more sensitized version of themselves. Venus romancing becomes more spiritualized; Mars becomes kinder and gentler; Mercury becomes more intuitive and psychic. Neptune dissolves.

Natal Neptune Example

My natal Neptune conjuncts Saturn in the 11th House. I tend to project a kind of social utopianism in that I see the highest potential in others, but not always their limitations. The utopian bubble I inhabit may not be of this world, yet its spirit lives on in the people I work closely with in the dream-based group dynamics of cinema, ritual, theatre, music and poetry. My greatest disappointments have come from friends and groups failing to live up to my big utopian dreams and expectations for them. Since Saturn also conjuncts Neptune, I have learned to replace these social expectations with more awareness of the limitations of others. This helps me follow only those dreams with enough real life-support to come true; I have no use for pipedreams. I am now *a reality-based dreamer.*

The Shadow of Neptune

When Neptune is over-emphasized, there can be a sense of being in the world *but not of the world.* Sometimes this other-worldly quality can lead to an inability to function in society, while other times it can inspire new ways of being in the world (but still not *of the world*). This shadow aspect can imbue individuals with a quality of vagueness, spaciness, and a kind of oblivious way about them. This distortion can also occur as apathy, listlessness and a withdrawal from external life. Some poets, artists and musicians who over-emphasize their Neptunes can live inspired lives and claim to be guided by Muses or Angels. Those living inspired lives can also overlook basic survival needs, schedules and personal hygiene; *the divine madness of poets who forget to bathe.*

The shadow aspect of the under-emphasized Neptune can distort as an absence of spiritual awareness and a corresponding over-identification with materiality. There can be a claustrophobic sense of being trapped in the physical body that can dramatize outwardly as a dread of being in small rooms or an irrational fear of elevators. In this shadow aspect, there can be a sad lack of imagination maintained by the tyranny of overly-literalist thinking. Intuition may be ignored or mistrusted. Without imagination and intuition when facing life's ever-present uncertainties, an otherwise natural fear of unknowns can turn someone into an anxious, hyper-phobic hypochondriac.

12th HOUSE—STATE OF THE SOUL

The Internal Landscape, Solitude, Spirituality

Twelfth house experience calls to our spiritual needs for solitude, solace and withdrawal from the external pressures of society, friends, career, school, relationships, work, family, etc. Meeting

Experiential Astrology

these needs provides a sense of sanctuary or a temporary escape from harsher, more difficult realities we are asked to endure. Sometimes 12th house experiences can point to more mystical states of escape, not *from* mundane reality, but escape *into* Reality. In the State of the Soul, the internal landscape of personal dreams, memories and repressions overlays with the dreams of the collective and deeper memory banks in the Akashic Records of human evolution and reincarnation.

In nocturnal dreams, the psyche processes daytime tensions, unchecked childhood traumas, and other psychic material innate to one's personal psychology. However, autonomous liminal presences and archetypal entities beyond our own personal history also visit our dreams. Conscious interaction with our dreams can support a healthier relationship between conscious ego and the subconscious. This can be initiated by keeping a dream journal, entering Jungian psychotherapy, or any artistic process involving receptivity to subconscious impulses and their expression as Art.

Psychologically, the 12th house acts as a kind of depository of the Subconscious Mind. Certain aspects of our personality that we are not ready to face or display to others are stuffed (repressed) in the Subconscious 12th house. The State of the Soul governor can indicate something about the aspect of personality that tends to get repressed. Those with Aquarius Rising and a Capricorn 12th state governor may repress their claim to authority. Scorpio at this cusp may repress sexuality. Those with Virgo Rising and Leo governing the 12th house might repress their childish creative impulses.

12th house experiences also include the wide spectrum of mental illness and the so-called "crazies" stuffed into society's own subconscious of psychiatric wards and prisons. Traditionally, the 12th house refers to organizations set apart from society such as rehab centers, hospitals, insane asylums, prisons, monasteries & nunneries, secret (esoteric) societies, and cults. 12th house planets refer to forces that remain out of conscious reach unless they can be excavated by introspection, meditation, yoga, holotropic breathwork and rebirthing, dance therapy, Paratheatre and body-based psychotherapies.

Balance Point (6th House)

Excessive self-withdrawal can overwhelm and "drown" the conscious ego in unintegrated subconscious complexes, unprocessed traumas, and isolation. 6th house experiences for being useful to others (service), putting things in order (organizing), finding employment, and learning new skills can alleviate the suffering of self-imposed isolation. Focus on service to a common good can defuse over-identification with 'psychological demons' and release the grip on the ego from the contents of the Subconscious.

ESSENTIAL RESEARCH TASKS

Experimenting with States, Forces & Styles

To test the plethora of theories, definitions and insights outlined in "The 12 Symbolic Families", the research tasks below can start providing opportunities for a more direct experience of the actual phenomena these astrological terms and symbols represent. Without experimentation, there can be no such thing as Experiential Astrology. Testing theories over repeated experiments can bring the results to determine their value. As more experiments are conducted, pattern recognition increases to support more informed astrological interpretations. Knowledge based on actual experience, not just what's read in books or heard secondhand, turns into wisdom.

The States: The Life Experience List

After reading "The 12 Symbolic Families", examine the history of your own actual life experience by identifying: **1)** the State representing *the least amount of life experience* and **2)** the State representing where you have had *the most life experience*. Then make a list with the State where you have the most experience at the top and the State you have the least experience with at the bottom. List the other States by degree of experience from the most to the least in between the first and last State. For some, this list may seem impossible at first. Stick with it as it can show you how you have prioritized the time of your life. As you engage more variety in life experiences, the sequencing of this list will change.

Renaming the States

After reviewing the 12 States, rename each of them with a word or phrase that defines the experience there for you at this time. Allow these phrases and names to change as you discover more about what each State represents.

Activating a Force

Choose one force (planet) that you feel could use more emphasis and integration in your daily life. Then look to your chart to see which state it's placed in and also, the style that governs that state (the house cusp). Experiment with entering that state through the style of governor to engage its experience. If you are committed to the experience, note how the force(s) activate(s). Repeat the experiment; write down the results.

Styles as Point of View

Each of the twelve styles (signs) express a distinct point of view. Choose one style each day for twelve days and experiment with seeing and responding through that style. This experiment can show you where your *blind spots* are by those styles you have the least understanding of or possible resistance to. Once you can identify a blind spot, you have a chance of learning something about yourself you didn't know before. This task can also show you which styles you have favored more than others, and as a result, have become biased by. Archetypal chauvinism! This experiment can open up multiple perspectives by perceiving many different angles to everyday situations. Prism consciousness.

HOROSCOPE EXAMPLES
Excerpts from Three Natal Readings

The following three charts belong to individuals who requested nonlocal readings from me. We did not meet in person. I recorded my interpretations alone and sent them to the clients as MP3 audio files. Before doing each reading, I asked the clients to send me questions and concerns that they would like me to address. Excerpts of their concerns are included after each of their charts. I follow their noted concerns with my responses based on clues discovered by tracking *The 12 Symbolic Sets,* as well as other methods presented in this book. (Client names, genders and birth data have been excluded to honor their privacy.)

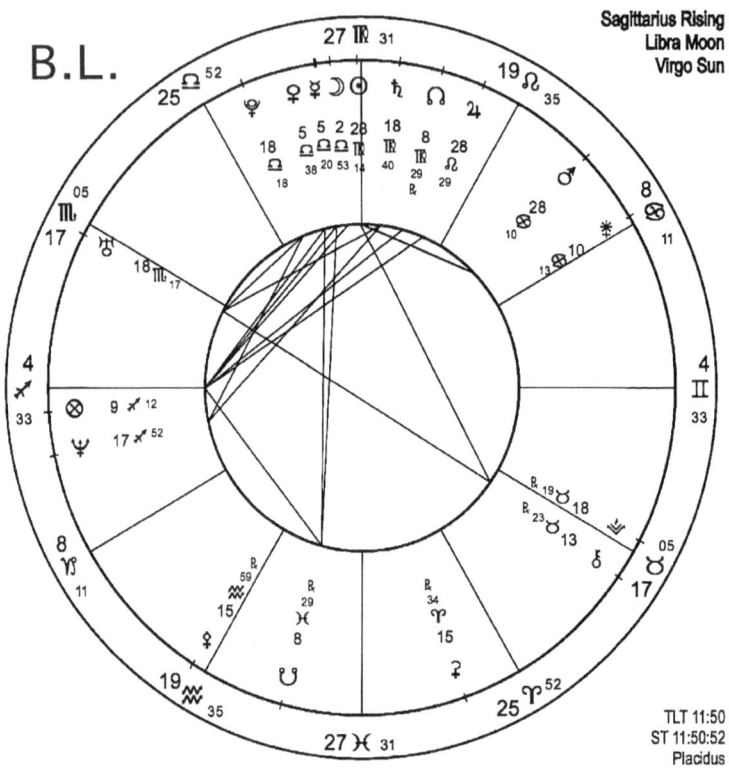

"I just overall feel very lost and directionless. I wish I could honestly say I had some detailed notion as to the purpose of having a reading, but I cannot honestly say I do. It is possible I am just clutching at straws, hoping somebody may be able to tell me something I need to hear. I quit a job in the tech field a few years ago, and am thinking about going to school to pursue a totally different path. I have also thought about opening a business in yet another completely unrelated field. I believe that I have many interests and passions, but nothing so concrete as to say it's definitely what I want. Like a 'jack of all trades master of none' type thing." — B.L.

A.A. responds:

The focus here looks like *career*. I get that you're feeling aimless and looking for a meaningful direction. The heavy concentration of forces in your Professional State tells me you may have defined yourself almost entirely by your career. That four of these five forces are in Libra suggests that you may be married to your work; meaning your capacity for relationship has been almost completely invested in achieving your professional goals and ambitions. This can eventually lead to great success, but also to a kind of despair born from encroaching isolation, like a feeling of the walls closing in. When over-emphasized, this Libra archetype can also distort as *indecision* and a kind of fence-sitting which can naturally feel directionless.

With Saturn in your State of Faith, you are responsible for structuring the experience of whatever purpose or meaning you need. This means committing more fully to your unique point of view and how you know truth. Without this commitment, you may feel immobilized by the fear of not knowing what to believe. This placement of Saturn in Virgo represents sharp powers of observation and a strong capacity for critical thinking. With your Virgo Sun conjunct your Virgo Midheaven, you are in the position to take the helm of your career in any direction as long as it serves *your vision*. The caveat? You must know what that vision is, and then you must fully commit to it.

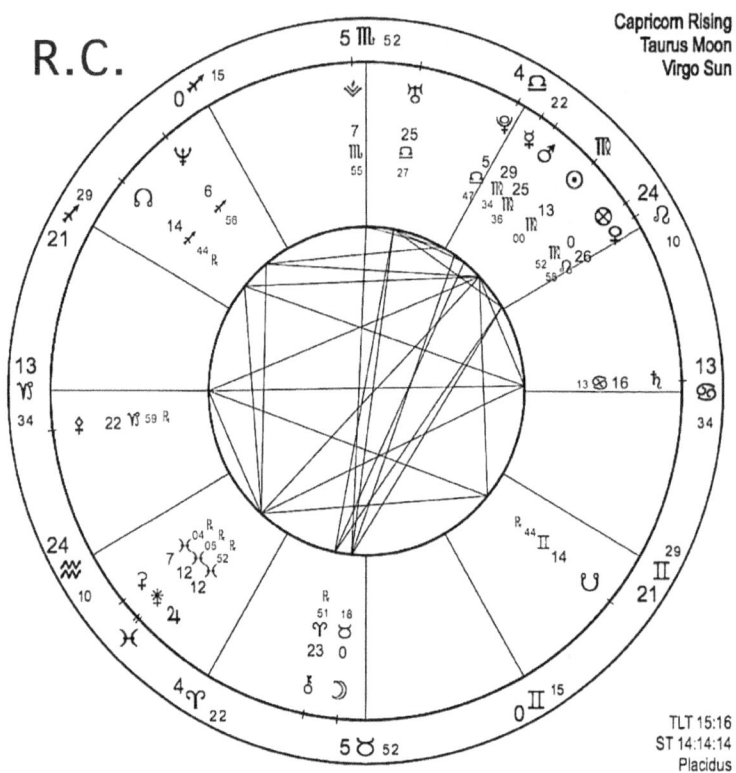

"Still really having a hard time with my relationship. I've never not had a hard time with my relationships though, and I don't know if that's just because I'm an asshole, they're an asshole, or if maybe I am just not the type of person who can feel safe intimately with people… It's always been a thing. Maybe it's all the trauma I've experienced in this life, or something I've been dragging around forever; if I choose the wrong people or I'm just not cut out for it… At any rate it's a massive issue which feels elusive and dead-ended for me." — R.C.

A.A. responds:

The focus here looks like *relationship*. With Saturn in your State of Intimacy, you may have very high standards around partnerships which can come with a fear of failure if those standards are not

Experiential Astrology

met. The first step is identifying what those standards actually are, and then asking yourself if you are playing a *double standard* by insisting that potential mates meet standards that you yourself have not yet met. You have to meet them first to be matched by someone who meets them. Saturn, in any chart, commonly points to an inherently difficult experience where personal effort and hard work are eventually rewarded with success over time; there's no overnight success story here. Your 7th house Saturn can indicate a successful relationship with someone who shares your goals and ambitions, and with whom you can accomplish more together than you could all by yourself.

Your Leo Venus in the State of Surrender screams sex, drugs and rock'n'roll, and so the relationship criteria here becomes complex, not simple. You want to rock out with a charismatic creative who's also together enough in their own life to help you realize your goals. I'm not saying it's impossible or that you don't deserve it, but you may be asking for a lot. The second step after identifying your high standards might be taking stock of what you have to offer a partner so that you don't focus too much on what you can or should get, and overlook what you have to share.

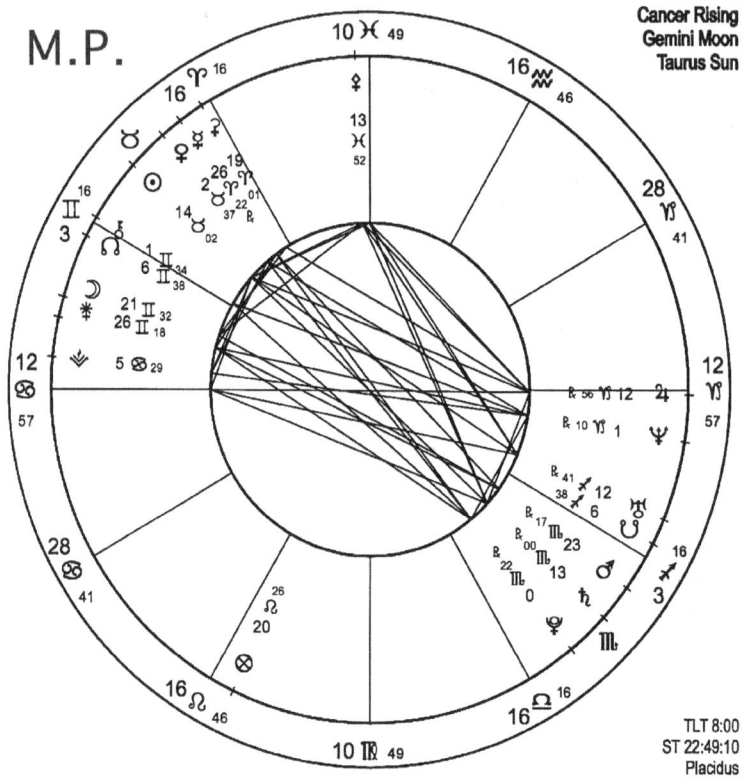

"The dream state is important to me, and has been since I was 7 and was lucid dreaming and journaling my dreams. Throughout my life I've experienced memory recollection from past lives within my dreams, as well as being able to astral project." — M.P.

A.A. responds:

The focus here looks like *dreams, past life memory, mysticism*. Every chart has a North Node representing the present life-calling, and the South node symbolizing the portal of past-life memory. The State of the Soul, or the 12th house, holds your North Node and Moon both in Gemini, symbolizing your experience of being called by, and into, the world of dreams. With the Sagittarius South Node, you may be approaching this dreamwork as a vision quest to give new meaning to your life. With Uranus conjunct that South

Node, also in Sagittarius, past lives were probably nomadic in nature to sustain a high level of freedom.

The 12th house North Node call to dreaming reverses the past-life trend of outer nomadic travel to the inner travel of astral projection and dreamwork. The 12th House Gemini Moon suggests that your present life-calling may also be tied to parenthood, family and settling down, as an evolutionary imperative to balance past-life focus of constant motion. With Pisces at the Midheaven, you may be able to bridge these inner experiences to the public through a career that inspires similar experiences in others. Neptune in your State of Employment suggests that your most effective vocation might be any line of work that *doubles as a mission* serving a transpersonal cause and not "just a job" that pays the bills.

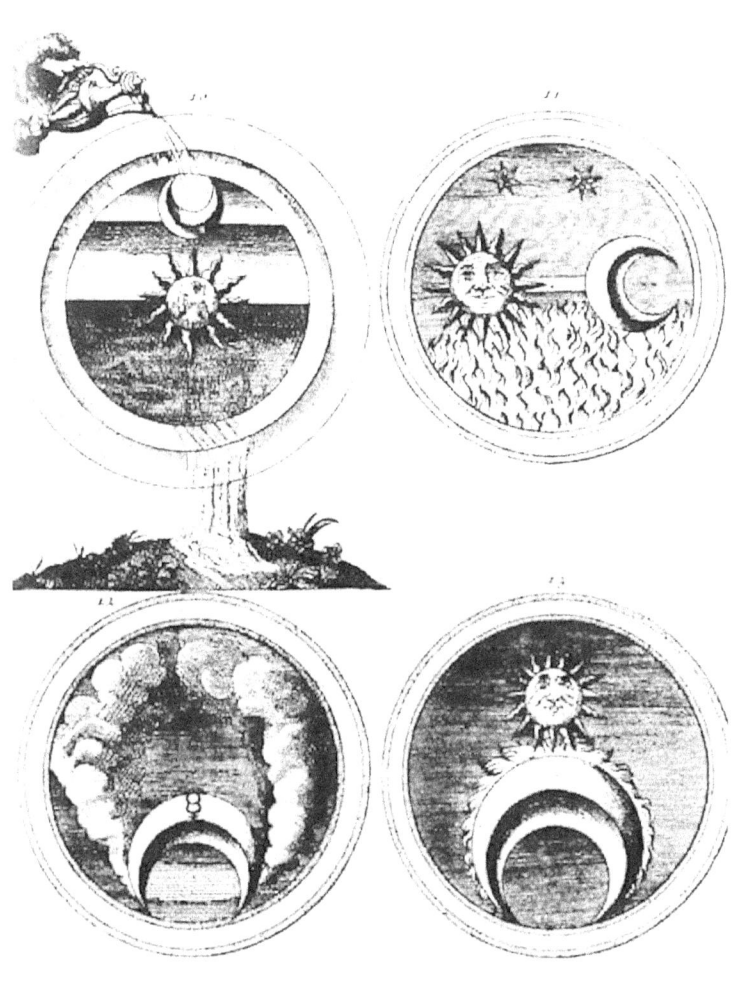

THEORY AND PRAXIS
The Nodal Axis, Asteroids, Chiron & Major Aspects

The Nodal Axis
Finding the Story in the Chart

SOUTH NODE (left) and NORTH NODE (right)

Every chart tells a story. I view the Nodal Axis of the South and North Nodes of the Moon as the story within the entire chart: a Big Picture vision of where someone came from (South Node/House), where they're going (North Node/House), and the tests and supports along the way (planetary aspects to the Nodal Axis). The Nodal Axis is also the first thing I look at when studying any horoscope.

The Science Behind the Moon's Nodes

The lunar nodes are the orbital nodes of the Moon; that is, the points where the orbit of the Moon crosses the ecliptic (which is the apparent path of the Sun across the heavens against the background stars). The ascending or north node is where the moon crosses to the north of the ecliptic. The descending or south node is where it crosses to the south. Eclipses occur only near the lunar nodes: solar eclipses occur when the passage of the Moon through a node coincides with the new moon; lunar eclipses occur when it coincides with the full moon. The lunar nodes complete a revolution through all the astrological signs (called a draconitic or nodical period) every nineteen years, also known as a Nodal Return. (Refer to the transiting Nodal Axis in the "Transits" section of this book.)

Fate vs. Destiny

Though many astrologers may disagree, I don't think astrology is, or can be, an actual science. I think it's more like a language and an art. The universe is not just made up of atoms, but of *stories*. And all the great stories are usually about *fate and destiny,* two words commonly confused to mean the same thing. Though related, they are not the same. I look fate as *our lot in life,* the circumstances we are born into. Some call it karma. Destiny, on the other hand, unfolds by how we respond to and relate with our fate. The choices we make inform our destiny. *Fate is in the cards; it's unknown until the cards are dealt. Destiny presents itself by how the cards are played.*

Opposing Orientations

The North and South Nodes are not planets or forces but represent specific orientations, indicating the past of our inherited fate (South Node) and the destiny (North Node) informed by our choices and responses to our fate. We come into this world with a series of overdeveloped (South Node) and underdeveloped (North Node) character traits. The South Node links us with the deep past (the current early life and previous incarnations) and symbolizes the character traits of our given strengths and innate talents—attributes that often come easy for us. When overemphasized, these familiar traits can produce a sense of redundancy, inertia, and an overriding feeling of being *stuck*. If and when the South Node (its sign and its state of experiences) becomes confused for our destiny, our chief purpose in the current life, we may find ourselves repeating the deep past and start spinning our wheels like a hungry tread-milling hamster.

The North Node (sign and house) symbolizes experiences we may find difficult or challenging due to undeveloped aspects in our personality (perhaps neglected in past lives). These novel North Node experiences, however, can evolve us so we do not constantly repeat the past. However, when overemphasized, North Node experiences can also stress us out with overwhelming novelty and personal growth. Over-emphasizing the North Node (sign and house) can become a crazy-making burnout scenario unless we retreat to the familiarity of the South Node where we can assimilate all the hot new information from the North Node frontlines of our existence. Aspects to the Nodal Axis can indicate specific tensions testing our resolve (squares), supportive harmonies (trines), and certain empowerments energizing and sometimes complicating our lives (planetary conjunctions to either Node).

The Purpose of Each Node

The true purpose of the South Node seems to be a kind of assimilation zone to process the novel experiences of the North Node. There is no leaving the South Node behind to try and live forever in the North Node zone; nobody escapes the past. Look at the Nodal Axis as a kind of dance between the South Node safety net of familiar habit patterns and the North Node's novelty-rich frontline edge of existence. The Moon's Nodes can also represent a deep spectrum of memory. Between past life memory and future memory—*who we have been and who we are becoming*—delineates a dimension both in and outside of time.

Future Memory

I learned about *future memory* while meeting an Australian Aborigine Koori elder who shared the way his people relate with what we call "time". For the Koori tribe, the future has already happened and needs only to be remembered to discover who we have already become. What we call "the past" in their world (which precedes most cultures by many thousands of years), *does not exist*. There is only the Ancestors of the eternal now who remain a constant presence in their daily lives and in their dreams.

Experiential Astrology

When I was first introduced to these new ideas about time, my big white mind spun like a swizzle stick in a cold stiff drink. It took me awhile to step back and consider aboriginal time as just as real as how the rest of the world knows time. This ancient model of time makes up but one thread in the tapestry of aboriginal spirituality based in what they call *Dreamtime*. Their Dreamtime is synonymous with how they know the Earth as a massive dreaming entity incarnating as this planet, constantly dreaming all living things into existence. It's easy to accept that when we sleep at night: we inhabit a dreambody that goes on adventures in dreamland. Now imagine, upon awakening, that same dreambody goes to sleep and starts dreaming you into existence as you rise the next morning and go about your day.

The Esoteric Nodal Axis

What does the aboriginal Dreamtime, the eternal ancestors, and future memory have to do with the Nodal Axis? It starts with the South Node as the only symbol in the horoscope that points to past life karma. Readers with trouble wrapping their heads around the three-thousand-year-old concept of past lives and reincarnation might approach this notion as a creative narrative, a colorful fiction wrapped in kernels of truth and mystery. It can be vexing to try believing something you haven't experienced yet. It takes a leap of *imagination and faith* to envision past lives, two valuable attributes in the Experiential Astrologer's toolbox. Imagination starts out as innocent child's play until it crosses the threshold into higher intelligence.

> *"Imagination is more important than knowledge. For knowledge is limited, whereas imagination embraces the entire world, stimulating progress, giving birth to evolution."*
> — Albert Einstein

Past Life Memory Portals

When we know how to do something very well without having been trained, maybe we think it's a talent inherited from parents. Or perhaps a past life? There are times we meet a stranger who seems oddly familiar and, after some conversation, we feel like we've known them and been known by them our entire lives. Or perhaps a previous lifetime? Beyond a deep reservoir of familiar talents, strengths and knowledge, the South Node also represents a kind of portal to past life memory. This portal opens up when we become aware of experiences, thoughts and insights that clearly did not originate in the present lifetime.

Past life memories can sometimes flood present time ego-consciousness with images and emotions creating confusion about present lifetime direction and purpose. This occurred to me in August of 2006, at the age of 53, when I felt a compulsion to google search monasteries under a fierce conviction that it was my time to become a monk. Very strange, since I had felt no monastic longing until that day. Yet for three days that summer, I was totally convinced that my life as I knew it was over, and monkhood was my true calling and destiny!

It wasn't until after I looked at the ephemeris that I noticed the transit of Saturn conjunct my 9th house Leo South Node—a red flag moment! I knew enough about the Nodal Axis to realize that if I mistook my South Node as my calling and destiny, I would become slam-dunked into a sinking mire of redundancy. Whoa! Turns out, I've already been a monk; *been there, done that*. What a relief. This was a Saturn reality check to turn around and face the future, not the past. My 3rd House Aquarius North Node calls out: *you have books of unsent messages to share.*

South Node Karma

Karma, as defined here, doesn't mean "good karma" or "bad karma" but simply the *consequences* of actions, experiences and orientations any life has taken on. Past life karma refers to consequences of actions, experiences and orientations that defined the life of the soul in the previous incarnation. I have come to understand how the current life starts with an overlay of past life karma as a way for the person to orient and acclimate to the new challenges of the present lifetime symbolized by the North Node.

The South Node initially helps us gain footing until we can grasp the current lifetime's evolutionary agendas, symbolized by the North Node style and state (and any forces within a six-degree orb). When we find ourselves overly fixated in the South Node area, past life memory can start flooding present time consciousness with old agendas and outdated programs. When South Node agendas dominate consciousness, we can start looping in redundant cycles of inertia, suffer familiarity overdose, and get stuck repeating the past. Any past life can be pictured by an accurate and imaginative interpretation of the style and the state of the South Node and any forces (planets) aspecting it within a six-degree orb.

When the North Node Calls

If the South Node refers to past lives, the North Node points to our future self or *who we have already become,* the one waiting for the rest of us to get up to speed. When a client asks me about their life purpose, or their "calling", I look at their North Node to get a picture of what that "calling" might look like. An accurate analysis of the North Node sign and its house requires an imagination for envisioning what the story might look like and the narrative that comes with it. The North Node may be one of the more misunderstood terms in the astrological alphabet.

In any predominately production-oriented society, one's "calling" is often associated with career. For some (with 6th or 10th house North Node or in Capricorn or conjunct Saturn), this can be relevant and true. For the rest of us, this impersonal cultural idea can lead to a confusing and even disastrous end if we base our entire futures on the mistaken assumption that career equals calling. It can be for some, but not all. It is entirely possible to have a career while also following a calling in parallel and separate fields. Sometimes the calling can be in conflict with career, depending on planetary aspects to the North and South Node.

The call of the North Node can be like a transmission of signals from a faraway place. It represents experiences that may differ wildly from any past life orientation and, as such, points to a path of difficulty. To follow the call of the North Node is to embrace the difficult. Yet all difficulty is not meaningful. Some are stuck in a life filled with a series of meaningless difficulties, whereas others choose to align with the difficulty that creates meaning in their lives. The North Node symbolizes a direction of meaningful difficulty. Though he was not an astrologer, I believe that's what the poet Rilke may have meant when he said:

"Most people have turned their solutions toward what is easy and toward the easiest of the easy; but it is clear that we must trust in what is difficult; everything alive trusts in it."
— Rainer Maria Rilke

Activating the North Node

When the North Node is activated, it can amplify the sense of purpose and forward-moving direction in life. The North Node can be energized by engaging the experiences linked with its house and the planet, or force, in the same symbolic family of the North Node sign. (Refer to "The Dispositor Planet" in the "Interpretive Techniques" section.)

For example, my Aquarius North Node belongs to the Aquarius, Uranus and 11th house set. I have known my sense of purpose and direction to increase after engaging group experience (11th house) and consciousness expansion events (9th house Uranus), often at the same time. This has not made my life any easier but it has made it more meaningful. I've experienced my 3rd house Aquarius North Node chiefly through the writing of my many books, a process that remains to this day the most difficult thing I know how to do. However, by doing the meaningful difficult thing, my life has actually become a whole lot easier.

North Node Exhaustion

The state and style of the North Node points to experiences of a highly novel and innately challenging nature, and can easily lead to the exhaustion of *psychic burnout* when these experiences are over-emphasized. The often-exhilarating North Node experiences of novelty can spin our lives like a swizzle stick in a cosmic cocktail of accelerating chaos. Getting stuck in the North Node area can be crazy-making in this way. The way to stop the madness is to retreat back to more familiar experiences, as symbolized by the state and style of the South Node, to process the hot new data absorbed on the cutting edge of our existence until we're ready to return and hit the front line, again.

Nodal Axis Research: Discover Your Story

The North Node can show something about where a life is headed. Understanding the nodes' specific conditions—its Signs, Houses, nearby Planets—can allow a more conscious participation in its actualization. The Nodal Axis is like a compass on a ship sailing the high seas of consciousness. A sense of forward-moving direction can be experienced by aligning with the North Node while using the South Node to steady the course as a rudder, when the lightning storms of novelty threaten to capsize your vessel. To discover your Nodal Axis story, interpret the South and North Nodes, the Signs and Houses they inhabit, and any aspects they share with planets, forming them into a narrative—a story with a beginning, a middle, and an end.

STEP 1): MAKE THE LIST. Make a South Node list and a North Node list. Write down specific activities and experiences pertaining to your understanding of the STATE and STYLE of your SOUTH NODE and your NORTH NODE.

TASK 2): DO THE EXPERIMENT. Set apart time to explore and experiment. Look at your list and find ways to engage the experiences and activities symbolized by your South and North

Nodes. You can include memories of what you have already experienced.

TASK 3): WRITE THE STORY. Write down the results of your experiences with both South and North Node areas and how you perceive the Nodes relating with each other. Using your imagination and firsthand experience as a foundation, compose a story about how you came into this world with certain gifts and abilities (South Node sign and its House), and how they might be used to face the tests and challenges of the current lifetime (North Node sign and its House). This story can be anywhere between 100 and 500 words.

The Author's Nodal Axis Story

9th House Leo S. Node (Conjunct Pluto)

Once upon a time, I was a charismatic cult leader with a loyal following during a long, lost era of nomadic caravan circuses. In our bizarre menagerie of sideshow acts, I was the Master Hypnotist. That is, until one stormy night, I was struck by a bolt of lightning which left me simultaneously enlightened and blind. The Master Hypnotist gave way to my new role as the Blind Seer, a popular circus freak that made me a famous fortune teller amongst the spiraling circus circuit. One day, I accidentally drank a glass of kerosene and burned out my vocal chords. I could no longer talk and was rendered a mute seer, a fate that ended my role in the circus. I was banished to the wilderness where the elements eventually had their way with me. With Pluto conjunct South Node, to move forward I have had to learn the correct use of will and power.

3rd House Aquarius N. Node (Conjunct Juno)

I was born into this life with an uncanny depth of intuition and philosophical insight that I credit to past life memory and experiences. This wisdom left me with the uneasy feeling that I would never be able to communicate everything I know within my deeper, yet very mute and introverted self. I was born with a 12th house Sun to minimize my past life grandiosity. Uncommonly at home in silence, as a teen I trained and then performed as a Mime Artist for ten years. This led to spoken theatre and ritual. I learned that it was not enough to simply know truth. Without the language to communicate my truths to others, I began spinning my wheels in isolation. Communication became a big deal to me, on par with survival needs of food and shelter. With Juno conjunct North Node, I have been married to my calling.

Nodal Axis Squared by Sun and Jupiter

My natal 18-degree Scorpio Sun and 15-degree Taurus Jupiter opposition *squares* my Nodal Axis (16 South Node Leo/16 Aquarius North Node). I've come to know this as a kind of emergency brake effect that informed a decision made in my fifties *to never rush*. With the exception of emergencies, where rushing may be essential to survival, I have since taken my time with whatever and whomever has come my way. In doing so, I experience this square to my Nodal Axis as a creative tension that clarifies my sense of purpose and also, when to retreat from the frontlines of my 3rd house back into my 9th house Leo South Node. Writing this book has been a North Node event while making films and music continue as South Node events.

The Four Major Asteroids
And Their Ancient Goddess Mythologies

Juno, Pallas, Ceres and Vesta

The four asteroids included here were discovered between 1801 and 1807 in the asteroid belt orbiting between Mars and Jupiter, along with thousands of other asteroids. These asteroids—*Juno, Vesta, Pallas, Ceres*—were not incorporated into Western astrology until sometime in the mid-20th century. Up until then, Western astrology only included planets linked with Masculine deities, with Venus and the Moon as sole (and soul) ambassadors of the Feminine. Named after ancient goddess mythologies, these four asteroids bring more gender balance to the horoscope. I first read about these asteroids in the book *Asteroid Goddesses* by Demetra George and Douglas Bloch (first published in 1985 and still in print). I highly recommend it.

Every culture shares their stories of gods and goddesses—*Greek, Roman, Egyptian, African and European*—to reflect their own eras and myths, sometimes with different names for the same archetype; i.e., Juno is also known as Hera, Pallas aka Athena. After a few years studying goddess mythologies from various cultures, I distilled my own visions of these four major asteroid goddesses for the horoscopes I was interpreting. The asteroids seem to hold more influence when either conjunct a chart's four corners—ASC, IC, DESC, MC—or conjunct/opposing the Moon, Mercury, Venus, Mars, Jupiter, Saturn or the Sun. Free-floating asteroids disconnected from these points don't seem to matter as much, though I could be wrong. I was startled to find all four asteroids in my own chart placed in highly strategic positions (conjunct ASC, conjunct Nadir, conjunct North Node, opposing Mars). *Oh, my Goddess!*

JUNO, The Power Couple

The Myth

Juno, aka Hera, was a powerful goddess married to Zeus, aka Jupiter, the so-called "god of the gods." Their powers were well-matched, allowing Juno to accomplish far more with Zeus than she could alone. She immensely enjoyed the *empowerment of marriage*. However, Zeus was a philandering god who chased the sylphs, mermaids, sirens and other mythic entities to satisfy his endless lust. His betrayal outraged Juno and though she was powerful enough to destroy Zeus, she knew it would end a marriage that she needed for her goddess work. She forgave Zeus while destroying his various mistresses, giving his wandering eye a reality check.

The Internal Marriage Archetype

Juno represents where *we may already be married,* where we show great tenacity and unending devotion. Like any marriage, there are certain conditions that sustain the marital bond. These conditions are symbolized by Juno's Style and the State she's in, along with any aspects with other Forces. When these conditions are neglected, *self-betrayal* can set in and the internal marriage wavers. If self-betrayal persists, it can dramatize externally in a betrayal of any significant external relationship with corrosive resentment, contempt and clandestine affairs.

The conditions of the internal marriage are made up of Juno's sign and house, namely, a sustaining of the experiences symbolized there. Conditions for a 10th house Juno includes tending to goals and ambitions. A 5th house Juno needs to stay creative, and a 12th house Juno needs her solitude. By sustaining the conditions of the internal marriage, Juno becomes a kind of template to measure compatibility in any potential external marriage or intimate partnership, depending on the degree the inner marriage is accepted and supported by both parties.

In spite of many positive elements in a given relationship—*friendship, great sex, shared interests, etc.*—if the internal marriage of either partner is dismissed, ridiculed or attacked, it can be a deal-breaker. I have seen this play out in many Synastry readings. When examining each person's Juno placement, I ask myself: *what is this person already married to? How does their partner relate with that? Are they supportive of this internal marriage or conflicted about it?* These are questions I also share with the client.

Example of What We May Be Married To

- Aries/State 1: to oneself, to one's own voice and view
- Taurus/State 2: to one's values, possessions, money
- Gemini/State 3: to one's ideas, learning, and talking
- Cancer/State 4: to one's family or clan, to the home
- Leo/State 5: to one's art or creativity, to children

Natal Juno Research

Locate natal Juno and see if and how there are any correlations between its placement and sign and your actual life experience with relationships. See if Juno indicates any kind of criteria for compatibility with potential mates and partners (including business partners); the deal-breakers and the deal-makers. Examine natal Juno for any sign of your own "betrayal issues" when the conditions of the internal marriage are neglected or dismissed and they arouse outrage, indignation, or wrath.

PALLAS, The Visionary Warrior

The Myth

Pallas, aka Athena, was a powerful warrior priestess goddess, famed and feared for leading her army into far more victories than defeats. As a devotee of the oracle Medusa, whose likeness she had ingrained on her battle shield to terrorize her foes, Pallas was also a Seer with a clear vision of what she was fighting for.

The Good Fight

Natal Pallas represents *a fighting spirit.* Its placement can indicate where we may need to put up a fight to advance. Pallas differs from the fighting spirit of Mars which tends to be more about fighting *against* something or someone. Pallas represents "the good fight" of knowing what is actually worth fighting *for* so that precious time and energy is not wasted fighting against whatever rubs the ego the wrong way. This shift from "fighting against" to "fighting for" brings focus and vision to the frontlines of any battle.

Example of Pallas & the Good Fight

- Virgo/State 6: fighting for doing the right thing
- Libra/State 7: fighting for equality
- Scorpio/State 8: fighting for change that makes a difference
- Sagittarius/State 9: fighting for one's truth
- Capricorn/State 10: fighting for goals that impact the world
- Aquarius/State 11: fighting for the community
- Pisces/State 12: fighting for consciousness itself

Natal Pallas Research

Locate natal Pallas and see if and how there may be correlations between its placement and a need for a more enlightened fighting spirit in that area. Perhaps this has been an area where too much passivity or victim trauma has inhibited the advancement of winning in this state. Pallas asks, *"What is worth fighting for?"*

CERES, The Great Mother

The Myth

Ceres, aka Demeter, was a powerful goddess of Agriculture and the mother of Persephone, aka Kore, a maiden archetype. One day, Persephone wandered the fields picking Narcissus flowers when she was abducted by Pluto, aka Hades, god of the Underworld, as his Child Bride. When word of this kidnapping reached Ceres, she grieved so heavily over the loss that all the crops of the land wilted. This alerted Zeus who immediately sent Hermes, aka Mercury, down to the Underworld with a message for Pluto to appear before Ceres and *negotiate a deal*. Pluto and Ceres met and finally agreed to allow Persephone to live with one of them for six months and then the other for the following six months, and so on. Though begrudged by the pact, Ceres was happy to have her daughter back for half of the year, and the crops of the land came back to life.

Trauma of Loss, Grief, Negotiation

Natal Ceres can represent a complex trauma point in the natal chart where there may be, or may have been, a significant loss followed by grief (repressed or expressed) as part of the ongoing healing process around this loss. Similar to Cancer or the Moon, Ceres represents a nurturing power of *sustaining care* when it comes to living with loss. An important part of this healing process continues as grief transforms through a reassessment—*the negotiation*—of how we can relate with and live with a specific loss and also, with loss in general as an integral part of life. In some instances, Ceres can represent a transformation of *tragic into magic.*

Natal Ceres Research

Locate natal Ceres and see if and how this area may be directly or indirectly linked with any significant loss in your life, and if so, whether the grief has been repressed or expressed. See if there has been a reassessment and negotiation with the self around this loss, or a need for it. As a mother archetype, Ceres can also indicate a psychological loss of the Child Within, buried (repressed) deep in the Underworld of the Subconscious, where self-negotiation may be needed to bring that Child back.

VESTA and the Temple of Hestia

The Myth

Vesta, aka The Vestal Virgins, were esoteric priestesses who maintained the Temple of Hestia, great goddess of the Hearth. These priestesses were not necessarily literal virgins, but Hestia-devotees living spiritual lives while cultivating the arts of music, literature, poetry and cuisine. Each was assigned a specific duty in the daily upkeep of the Temple. The most important responsibility was keeping *the sacred fires* of the Holy Hearth burning.

The Experience of Sacredness

Natal Vesta can indicate where and how we can come to know *an experience of the sacred* in our lives and the kinds of processes (Vesta's State, Style, planetary aspects) that can keep that sacred flame alive. What's sacred can be relative to each chart and person. Arguments may appear between individuals with Vestas squaring each other about what constitutes "the true sacred"; what is sacred to one, can be profane to another.

Natal Vesta Research

Locate natal Vesta to see if and how this area corresponds with your own subjective experience of the sacred and the conditions required to sustain or feed the sense of sacred in your life—how to keep the flame alive. These conditions are encoded into Vesta's sign and house.

Comet Chiron & Punk Rock
Self-Sabotage and the Force of Subversion

Chiron orbits between Saturn and Uranus as their unruly love child, a wild conglomeration of responsibility and freedom. In the physical body, Saturn symbolizes the skeletal system; Uranus, the electrical system; and Chiron, the interactions between them. This can be seen in the example of chiropractors treating patients by manipulating the interactions between the spine (SATURN) and the Central Nervous System (URANUS). Chiron mediates between Saturn's structural integrity and Uranus' electrical power.

Chirotic (rhymes with erotic) eruptions can arouse the coiled serpent of *kundalini* in the root of the spinal cord to rise through the spine, activating energy centers (chakras), while transforming the sympathetic and parasympathetic nervous systems. This can occur spontaneously without warning. Kundalini can also be intentionally activated through the practice of Kundalini yoga.

Chiron can indicate a latent talent for creating hybrids and ways of doing things that don't conform to the *status quo* yet can still function effectively in the world. Chiron the Maverick, Chiron the Outsider, *Chiron the Punk?* Punk rock. Chiron was discovered and named in 1977, the same year Johnny Rotten and the Sex Pistols' punk band sabotaged pop music and the fashion industry with their feral, primitive performances, their ragged punk aesthetic, and a DIY (Do It Yourself) ethos that persists to this day.

Self-Sabotage

In her book, *Chiron: Rainbow Bridge Between Inner & Outer Planets* (1987; Bear & Co.), Barbara Hand Clow defined Chiron as the "wounded healer." After I read the book I asked myself: *What wound? How does it happen and what does she mean by healing?* Though I found no specific answers to these questions in Clow's book, I also felt there had to be more grit to Chiron's story than the "New Age Wounded Healer." After studying many examples of natal Chiron in the charts I was reading, I started seeing how natal Chiron indicates where (the State) and how (the Style) we tend to unwittingly undermine and subvert our intentions. The wounding! Self-victimization! *We do it to ourselves, unwittingly.*

Until this undermining, self-stabbing pattern can be exposed, accepted and transformed, natal Chiron continues to symbolize a point of *self-sabotage*. Transforming this habit necessitates its exposure and an ongoing integration of the subversive force of Chiron. This means finding ways to *embody the Chirotic force* and become an agent of subversion through the state Chiron inhabits. The healing! *It's where we can do it ourselves, on purpose.*

What I mean by "subversion" is the creation of *alternatives* to the *status quo*. It's not about destruction for the sake of destruction, which only leads to a dismal, dreary, boring endgame. True subversion is about the *creative destruction* (Uranus) of *consensus reality constructs* (Saturn) to create space for alternative versions that undermine *status quo* models or definitions of the realities symbolized by Chiron's sign and house.

Knowledge of all twelve States seems paramount to grasping the nature of Chiron in any chart. When attempting to adapt or conform to mainstream definitions of experiences symbolized by Chiron's house, we can trip over ourselves and get in our own way. Until Chiron can be integrated, there can be a humiliation of failed attempts to conform to the *status quo* in an area (Chiron's house and sign) where conforming consistently fails. As Chiron becomes more integrated, we become as intentional saboteurs, consciously subverting consensus realities by offering alternative visions and definitions. *Subvert or be subverted.*

Chiron Examples of Subversion

- 2nd State: subverting mainstream models of security
- 4th State: subverting traditional family values
- 7th State: subverting *status quo* definitions of marriage
- 11th State: subverting social standards of group purpose

My Chiron Example

My natal Capricorn Chiron in the 3rd State of Mind symbolizes an embarrassing *foot in mouth* habit I've had every time I've attempted to learn or teach at a respectable institution or school. It also happens if I start writing or speaking in ways to try to impress others. I'm simply not cut out for the respectable, mainstream, *status quo* intellectual world. Integrating Chiron has meant becoming a more conscious force of subversion in the areas of thinking, language, learning and speaking.

Changing the key astrological terms of Planets, Houses and Signs into *Forces, States and Styles* won't change the world of Astrology, but it makes sense to me as an alternative, *or subversive,* way to rethink what these terms might actually mean. Redefining "success" (Capricorn) *in my own terms* also plays a key role in my Chiron integration. Every attempt to conform to society's ideas of success and career has left me feeling humiliated and wondering, "What was I thinking?"

CHIRON TASK: Sabotage the Saboteur

Locate your natal Chiron and identify your own patterns of self-sabotage. Observe and expose any unconscious or conscious attempts to conform to mainstream consensus models of how things "should be done" in that house. Then, discover or create alternative approaches and models to reclaim that house as your own. How would you like to act as a conscious force of subversion? Chiron's style (sign) offers a clue. What *status quo* ideas or beliefs or structures in Chiron's house are worth subverting?

The Six Major Aspects
Featuring the Charts of Seven Stars

Astrologers typically don't agree on precise universal measures to define the aspects, or angles, shared between planets; some use looser orbs, others use tighter orbs. I prefer drawing my orbs tighter to show the essential geometry, or crystal, of the horoscope often obscured by the spider-webbing effect of too many lines. With aspects involving the transpersonal forces of Uranus, Neptune and Pluto, I allow a slighter wider orb of maybe 8 or 9 degrees. Otherwise, all my orbs are set to 6 degrees or under.

I will not cover the so-called minor aspects of quintiles, semi-sextiles, septiles and noniles here. The focus will be on Conjunctions, Sextiles, Trines, Squares, Oppositions and the Quincunx. These six major aspects are accompanied by charts of six famous individuals along with my interpretations of their dominant aspects. A seventh chart of Bob Dylan is added to demonstrate a more compressive study of how multiple aspects can define an entire horoscope.

THE CONJUNCTION: A Fusion of Forces (Within 4 Degrees Orb)

When planets and points (ASC, MC, DESC, IC, the Nodes) are united within a 4-degree orb, they can blend together as a new energy or spirit. Complex conjunctions involving three or more forces and more than two conjunctions may represent a compound synthesis, and can indicate a certain talent for combining incongruous juxtapositions to discover hybrids, new models and ideas. Accurate translation of conjunctions requires a kind of alchemical or creative thought process to discern their distinct qualities while imagining what their combined outcome might look and feel like. Even simple conjunctions of two planets in different signs can require a more imaginative approach. It's a bit like cooking a stew and wanting to taste all the different ingredients.

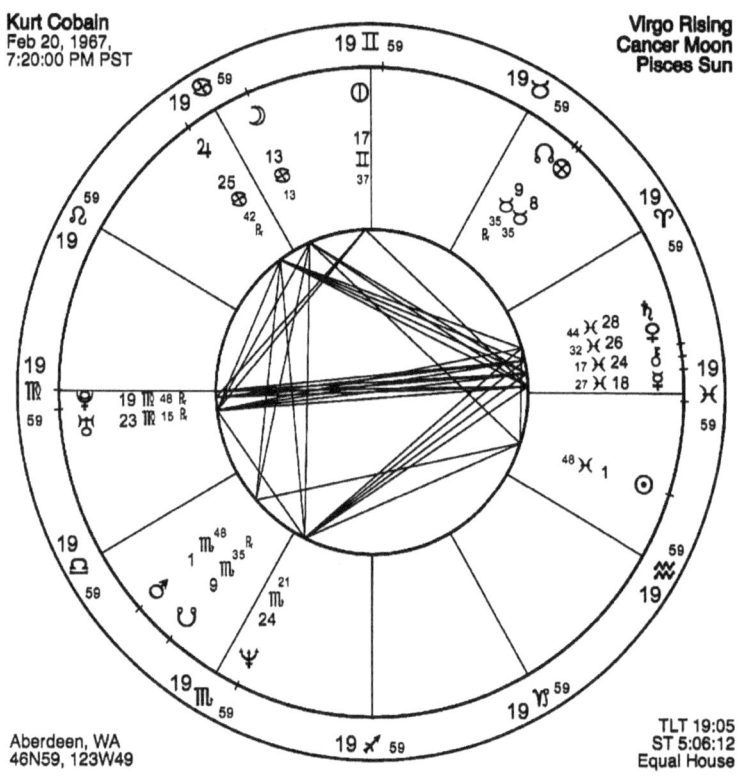

The Cultural Impact of Kurt Cobain

The *powerhouse conjunction* of Pluto, Ascendant and Uranus all in Virgo symbolizes a potent, charismatic voice of an entire generation. Though he was Gen-X, generations since continue resonating with his music, his lyrics and his anti-rock-star persona. Saturn and Venus conjunct in Pisces in the 7th State of Intimacy signals a serious artist whose work was put to task through the opposition shared with his powerhouse Virgo conjunction, igniting cultural dynamite that transformed the course of contemporary music with his band, Nirvana. This same Saturn/Venus conjunction may have also symbolized Cobain's aversion to fame. Note also the grand water trine—Jupiter, Neptune, Venus/Saturn—indicating a strong fluidity of emotional truth and honesty.

Experiential Astrology

THE TRINE: *Harmony Between Forces*
(120 Degrees of Separation; Within 4 Degrees Orb)

Planets trining each other share a strong harmonious flow. Trines can also indicate a natural talent the person may be unaware of *as a talent,* especially if it's experienced by them as "second nature." Trines represent areas that often come easy for us. A trine-dominant chart can indicate conflict-avoidant behavior and a tendency to keep things on the easy.

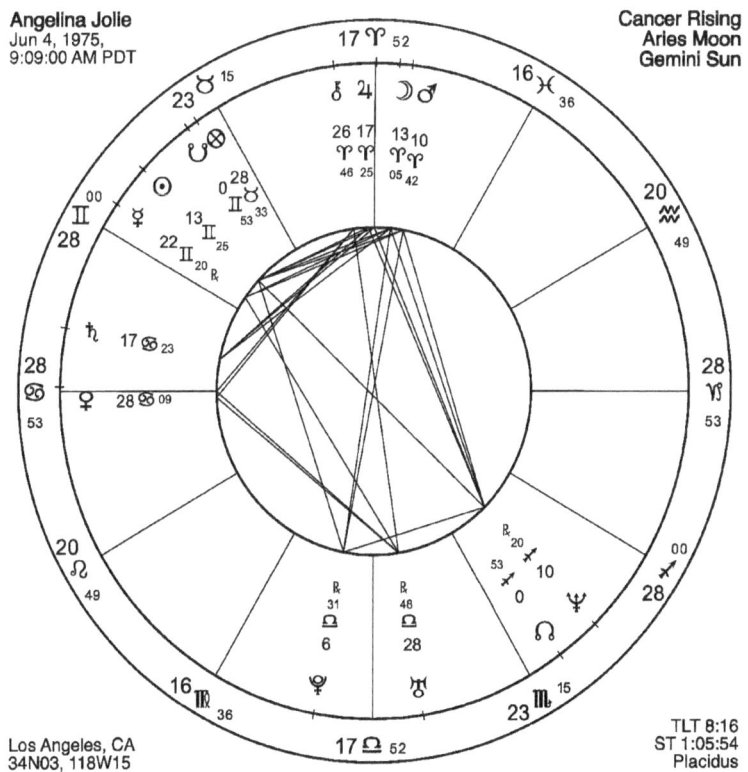

The Fierce Grace of Angelina Jolie

A *strong harmonious flow* symbolized by *the trine* between Neptune in the 5th Creative State and Mars/Moon conjunction in

Aries in the 9th State of Perspective speaks to the powerful state of grace Angelina inhabits throughout many of her films, especially the more action-oriented roles where she often performs her own stunts. The opposition shared between this Mars/Moon conjunction and her Pluto in the State of Mind suggests that playing these roles may be life-changing for her. Angelina may choose her roles not just for the money, but for what she can learn and what new skills she may have to train for to do the role. Note how Venus in Cancer closely conjuncts the Ascendant symbolizing an effortless embodiment of feminine and maternal beauty.

THE SEXTILE: An Alliance Between Forces
(60 Degrees of Separation; Within 3 Degrees Orb)

This aspect of allegiance shared between planets conveys an easy communication between their forces, as if they already agree with each other. Like friends talking on the phone, a shared support develops, grows and deepens over time through the sextile angle. An often-overlooked aspect, the sextile can provide a hidden foundation of internal support to assist other more challenging aspects in the chart.

There's no drama or conflict in sextiles—no big energy transfer or dynamic feelings. Sextiles serve a linking purpose. Like the lines connecting the knots on a fishing net, they represent strength as flexibility and support. Charts with three or more sextiles can represent those individuals who appear to others as having an easier life. That is, until the absence or avoidance of stress and conflict catches up with them when they become more easily overwhelmed by everyday survival struggles.

Experiential Astrology

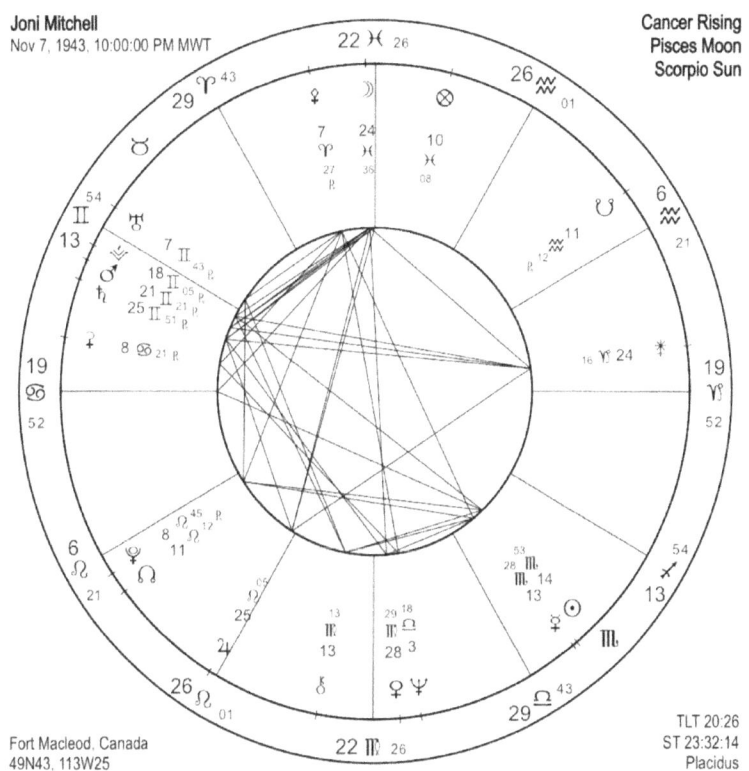

Joni Mitchell's Creativity Engine

Ms. Mitchell's chart shows a complexity of numerous aspects working together as a kind of multi-tiered creativity engine. Starting with the double sextile shared between her 12th House Gemini Mars/Saturn conjunction and her Jupiter in Leo (on the 3rd House cusp), her creative process initiates (Mars) and takes form (Saturn) in the subconscious (12th House). The sextile with Jupiter represents a *bringing forth* of the unconscious into conscious expression, what Carl Jung has called the *active imagination* for making the unconscious, conscious.

The double square shared between her 10th House Pisces Moon and her 12th House Gemini Mars/Saturn conjunction amplifies this *bringing forth* process as the depth of her innermost experiences are brought to the light of day through her lifelong commitment to public performance. The opposition her Moon shares with her 4th House Virgo Moon and Libra Neptune amplifies this further by how she shares the experiences that sustain her soul (4th House) in her songs with the impersonal public at large (10th House).

The powerful and dynamic square shared between her 2nd House Pluto in Leo and her 5th House Mercury and Sun conjunction in Scorpio represents an ongoing tempering of her creative impulses (5th House) to remain loyal to her values (2nd House) for staying creative (2nd House Leo governor). Since Pluto and Scorpio are in the same set, or family, this makes for what I call a friendly square, or a creative conflict.

Experiential Astrology 145

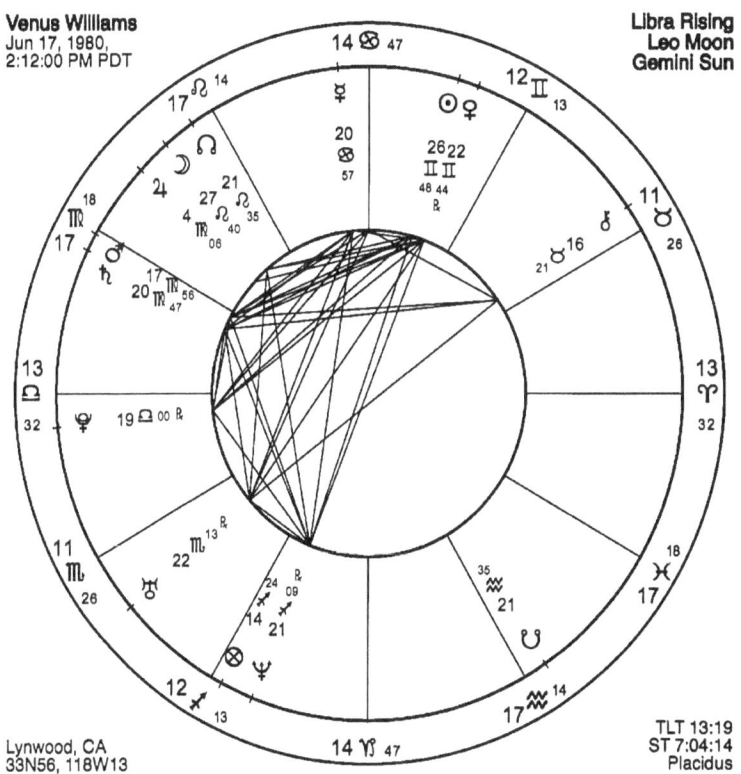

The Triumph of Venus Williams

The *multiple squares* from Gemini Venus/Sun conjunction in her State of Perspective and from her 3rd house Neptune to her 12th house Saturn/Mars conjunction creates *a complex T-square configuration*. This constellation of forces symbolizes a kind of combustible, energy-generating engine that seeks constant release through her 6th State of Employment. As long as Venus can work and/or stay useful in service of some kind, these strong inner tensions can be transformed by a powerful force of disciplined action (Saturn/Mars). Her Saturn/Mars in the 12th State of the Soul can also indicate a sensitivity to over-exposure in the public and a need for periodic withdrawal to stay sane. Whoever named her at birth may have known astrology, seeing how her Sun, the focal point of identity, is married to (conjunct) Venus. Whether or not they did, Venus was well-named.

The OPPOSITION: An Interplay of Contraries (180 Degrees of Separation; Within 6 Degrees Orb)

Oppositions are not "bad" aspects. There are no "bad" aspects, only difficult ones. This aspect refers to a kind of bridge between two opposing sides. This does not refer to any schism or split in the psyche. It's more like an interplay of contrary forces innate to our being. Oppositions symbolize confrontations and encounters within ourselves, while exposing our contradictory natures towards greater self-acceptance. These oppositions act like the negative and positive polarity of a psychic battery, where energy oscillates between opposite poles to generate power. Oppositions signify an ongoing confrontation with the self in specific ways (Planets & Signs) and areas (Houses). When these confrontations are ignored or avoided, they can dramatize outwardly through face-offs with individuals, groups and entire societies representing aspects of our own nature that we fail to face *on our own time*.

Experiential Astrology

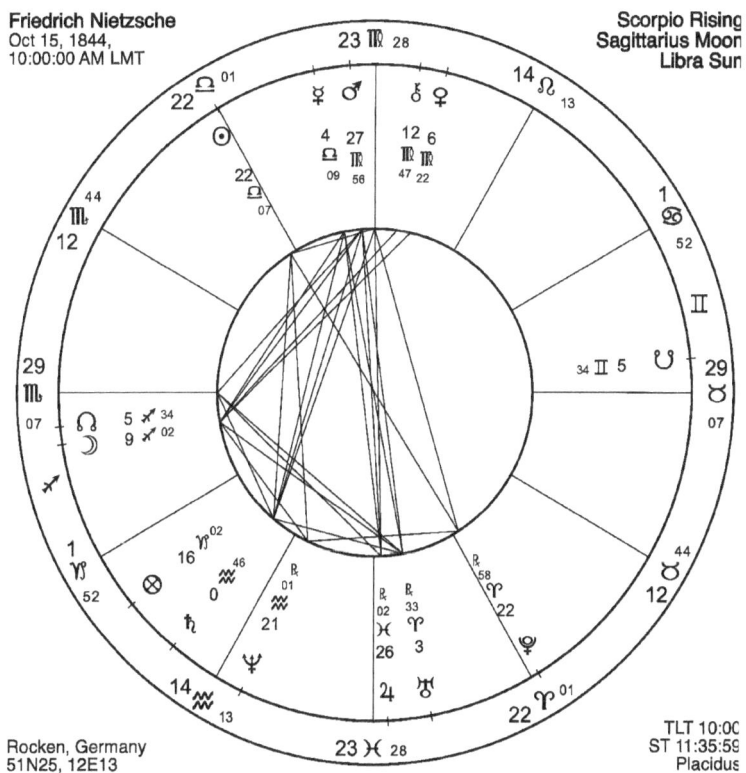

The Tragedy of Friedrich Nietzsche

It is rare for any chart to have more than two oppositions (not including the Nodal Axis). Here, *three separate oppositions* symbolize the ongoing struggle, brilliance and eventual madness of a great philosopher: Sun opposes Pluto, Mars opposes Jupiter, and Mercury opposes Uranus. Nietzsche's identity (Sun) underwent a lifelong process of self-transformation through a realization of *the will to power* (Pluto) as documented in his books. With Mars in his Professional State opposing Jupiter in the Sustaining State, *the will to power* was not pursued as any "armchair philosophy" but a vision to be acted on and made public. Mercury opposing Uranus indicates a genius capacity for processing experience and information very rapidly, often at speeds that left his contemporaries in the dust. This same genius may have also contributed to his getting so far ahead of his time that he could no longer relate to his present circumstances, resulting in eventual mental breakdown.

THE QUINCUNX: The Catalyst & the Catalyzed (150 Degrees of Separation; Within 4 Degrees Orb)

This elliptical and elusive aspect symbolizes a need for constant adjustment between the planets sharing the quincunx. This adjustment can be quite specific in that one planet tends to act as *the catalyst* to the other planet which acts as *the catalyzed*. In this dynamic, the catalyzed planet (force) undergoes a change to evolve itself. If the catalyzed force resists the changes triggered by the catalyst force, frustration and misfiring can occur between these forces, resulting in a kind of short circuiting. When the catalyzed forces stop resisting, they undergo a necessary change and order is restored.

The Catalyst and The Catalyzed

Catalyst		Catalyzed
ARIES	———>	VIRGO
TAURUS	———>	LIBRA
GEMINI	———>	SCORPIO
CANCER	———>	SAGITTARIUS
LEO	———>	CAPRICORN
VIRGO	———>	AQUARIUS
LIBRA	———>	PISCES
SCORPIO	———>	ARIES
SAGITTARIUS	———>	TAURUS
CAPRICORN	———>	GEMINI
AQUARIUS	———>	CANCER
PISCES	———>	LEO

Experiential Astrology   149

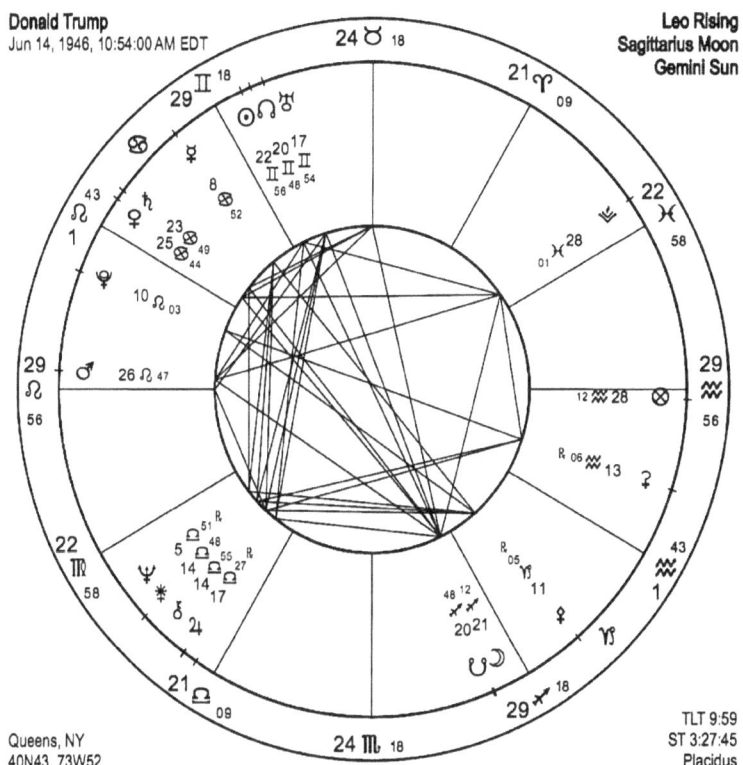

The Redundancy of Donald Trump

The elliptical *quincunx* angle shared between Mr. Trump's 4th house Sagittarius Moon/South Node conjunction and his 11th house Cancer Saturn/Venus conjunction represents a challenging and potentially vexing relationship with society, and especially, with women. The Moon/South Node conjunction represents a past life and present life childhood defined by a highly sheltered, entitled and overly-privileged lifestyle. The Saturn/Venus conjunction in his Community State symbolizes an early fear of "the common people" informing his efforts to fit into society by a growing commitment to use others and various groups to achieve his personal ambitions. *The Sociopathic Opportunist.* With his Saturn/Venus conjunction in Cancer, his process of maturing as a person depends on a deepening commitment to actually caring about other people. *What went wrong?*

In this example of a *frustrated* quincunx, Trump's over-identification with the privileged South Node/Moon resists the Cancer Saturn/Venus conjunction. Donald's maturation is stunted by his ongoing infantile reactions to *not always getting his way*. By also refusing to accept full responsibility for the consequences (Saturn) of his treatment of others, especially women (Venus), this quincunx reversal *backfires* into the personal chaos and social disruption that shadows Trump wherever he goes. As he keeps over-emphasizing the "privilege karma" of his South Node/Moon, Trump succumbs to a downward spiral of inertia, irrelevance and redundancy.

FOLLOWING THE MUSES CALL
Major Aspects in Bob Dylan's Horoscope

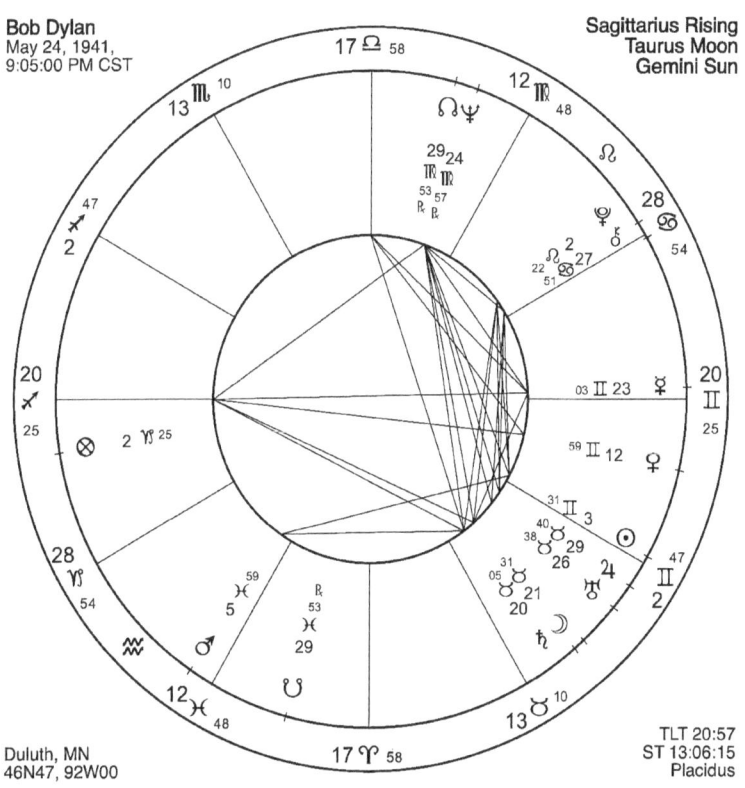

Neptune Conjunct North Node

Throughout his life Dylan underwent numerous stages of religious conversion and philosophical transformation that defined his life journey as symbolized by his 9th house North Node/Neptune conjunction. His 3rd house Pisces South Node refers to a past life and present life foundation as a wordsmith and poet. His sense of forward-moving destiny, however, was always tied to a spiritual quest. Hearing the call of the poetic and musical muse of Neptune, he aligns with his destiny of following his dreams and visions.

Neptune/North Node Trines
Saturn, Moon, Uranus, Jupiter (All in Taurus)

Dylan's ongoing spiritual quest harmonized with and fueled the multiple forces in his 5th Creative State, energizing his artistic development without conflicting with his spirituality. This multiple trine of earth-sign planets enables Dylan to manifest his quest to unprecedented success in the material world. In Taurus, this entire process becomes deeply aligned with his personal values.

Neptune/North Node
Squares Mercury in Gemini

Despite all his success and widespread fame, his thinking processes remained in an ongoing argument with it all. He may not have been at peace with the fruits of his labors in his continual intellectual dissent of his worldly recognition and all its accolades. This critical dissent may have also kept him in touch with his roots as a wordsmith and poet (Pisces South Node in the 3rd house); the skeptical eye, the ornery old man...

Gemini Sun Squares Mars in Pisces

This symbolizes an ongoing conflict of interests between running the day to day multimillionaire business of being Bob Dylan and the spiritual values motivating him. Mars, the Doer, represented Dylan's ongoing excitement with touring his band, a vital source of sustaining value, income and worth in his life. On the road, his spiritual quest takes on a powerful visceral immediacy that keeps him motivated and energizes his life purpose. Meanwhile, he can be nagged by the mounting details of keeping up with Bob Dylan, the Business (Mars square 6th house Gemini Sun), for preserving the quality of his big life.

Pluto in Leo Quincunxes Mars in Pisces

This quincunx symbolizes how the powerful transformations (Pluto) Dylan undergoes in his lifetime are actually meant to serve

Experiential Astrology 153

and fuel his motivation and the actions he takes. What he does (Mars) with this power is more important than the power itself. Here, we witness the conversion of archetypal transpersonal power (Pluto) into worthwhile actions (Second house Mars) as Dylan acts as a conduit for sociopolitical collective transformation (Pluto). Performing and touring his songs becomes a potent outlet for these larger forces that energize his North Node/Neptune, keeping him aligned with his destiny as a visionary minstrel.

ASPECTS RESEARCH: Writing Assignment

Using your own chart as a case study, write up your interpretations of two major aspects. Include real-life examples to validate your interpretations.

INTERPRETIVE TECHNIQUES
For the Investigative Astrologer

Intercepted Houses and Empty Houses

Intercepted Houses

More often than not, a House starts with one sign, the house cusp or governor, and ends with the next sign. Intercepted houses are those states containing three styles, or signs, within it. Horoscopes drawn for those born near the north and south poles can have four signs inhabiting a house, creating a more complex intercepted house. With every intercepted house, whether it's with three or four signs, the opposite house will also have three or four opposing signs in it. Charts with intercepted houses will also contain other houses that have only one sign that starts and ends that house. These one-style houses convey a simple and more singular frequency coloring the experiences represented there.

I will first share this *interception technique* with houses that contain three styles and then share some notes on those rarer charts with houses containing four styles. As a writer of fiction-based screenplays for feature art films, I've discovered how the three-sign combination in any intercepted house mirrors the basic story structure of *a beginning, middle and end.* In the intercepted house, a story starts through a particular style and passes through a second middle region (the second style) on its journey towards a destination in the third style. The middle region typically presents a crisis point that must be overcome to reach the destination point of the third style. Grasping the story within any intercepted house requires imagination and a rudimentary knowledge of *all twelve styles.*

Example: My Intercepted House Stories

In my natal horoscope, the 9th and 3rd states are intercepted. The 3rd State of Mind starts in Capricorn, moves through Aquarius, and ends in Pisces, symbolizing my writing process quite accurately. My writing projects, whether books or screenplays, always start as a goal-oriented endeavor. I rarely write anything unless it will be published online or as a book or magazine or as a screenplay for a film to be produced. Mars in Capricorn! Once into the writing process itself, Aquarius invariably creates a detour into a more experimental style than the more conventional style (Capricorn) I started with. If I resist Aquarius, I experience "writer's block." If I don't resist this newer unexpected direction, Pisces takes over and my writing flows more freely through deeper waters. This is how I find the emotional truth of whatever story I'm writing—after deviating from my Capricorn plans into the Aquarius detour towards Pisces.

My 9th house starts in Cancer, passes through Leo, and ends in Virgo. Along the way, I meet Uranus in Cancer, Pluto and South Node in Leo, and Virgo Moon. The 9th house feels more akin to my screenplay process. I feel my way through Cancer by discovering a vision worth caring about. This vision often arrives unpredictably from beyond myself, perhaps from the Muse of Uranus in Cancer. Following this vision, I fall into the past-life portal of the Leo South Node/Pluto and go on an ego trip. That's the crisis. I become deluded into believing I am the creator of this cinematic vision when it never really came *from me* but from the Muse of Uranus. When I'm lost in the sauce of ego, I hear the call from my Aquarius North Node: *Detach! Let go of ego!* If I can get my attention off myself and move forward into Virgo, I find comfort in the Moon. By serving instinct rather than my previously bloated creator self-image, the screenplay seems to start writing itself.

Four Signs in a House

Intercepted houses that include *four signs* are more rare since there are far fewer people living near the north and south poles than anywhere on the planet. Individuals fated with charts carrying four signs in two of the houses may have more complex stories to live through. I have only seen and read about a dozen of these extreme charts. The best interpretation I can offer is a 4-part narrative for each house containing four signs. These create a story structure that doesn't resolve like the 3-part story. It's more like the structure of a never-ending story, perhaps mirroring the more extreme, timeless spirit of the planet's polar caps.

Empty Houses?

Empty houses have no symbols in them. I'm often asked why there are empty houses in someone's chart, as if they might reflect some inadequacy on their part. I interpret the empty houses as *an inadequacy of astrology* to track forces in all areas equally. The empty houses simply refer to areas where we were not born to know what astrological forces are activated there and maybe for good reason—if horoscopes are purposeful, which I believe they are. Transits passing through these empty states can indicate a temporary activation of energies that ordinarily would not be present there. The governor of these empty states, the house cusps, take on extra influence. Much can be determined about any empty state by the characteristics of its governing style and the accompanying force, planet, in its symbolic set.

Mercury Logosis and The Venusian Dilemma

Mercury Logosis

This technique requires a discernment between what we know (Mercury) and who we are (Sun), between the idea-generating intellect of Mercury and the Sun as the mystery of being. Natal Mercury is placed either one sign behind the Sun, in the same sign as the Sun, or one sign ahead of the Sun. When Mercury is one sign behind the Sun, it can suggest a weaker capacity to articulate oneself. Finding words to explain or describe our perspective may be challenging, or maybe slower than we'd like it to be. This may not indicate a lower I.Q., but rather an innate sense that one's ideas are somehow behind one's being. It can be like understanding something without knowing it as firsthand experience. With this Logosis, there can also be a nostalgia for the past or a thinking and speaking style that favors the past tense.

When Mercury is in the same sign as the Sun, there can be an identification with ideas, a process accentuated when Sun and Mercury are conjunct in the same sign. *I think therefore I am.* This can be a challenging position when others critique our ideas and sources of information, and we experience our very being criticized or subject to dismissal. Of course, the being in and of itself remains beyond criticism as it inhabits a singular point beyond dualistic thinking. The Mercury/Sun conjunction can symbolize the mental habit for confusing our ideas for who we are.

When Mercury is placed in the sign ahead of the Sun, the intellect tends towards more forward-thinking without the mental baggage of identifying with any ideas it entertains. Ideas are viewed as autonomous agencies that light and leave, from mind to mind, like honeybees over fields of clover. There can be instances of prescience and even prophecy with this placement, where future outcomes can be seen and predicted.

The Venusian Dilemma

The placement of natal Venus determines how the magnetic force of personal love can be experienced. The experience of love to one person can be something else altogether to another, depending on the style and state Venus is in. This difference of Venusian styles can account for misunderstandings and conflicts in relationships where either party insists that their notion and definition of love is more valid than the other's. Love can be so dogmatic at times. Natal Venus is always placed either one or two signs behind the Sun, in the same sign as the Sun, or one or two signs ahead of the Sun.

When Venus is behind the Sun by one or two signs, affections may be slower to rise or less accessible to oneself. Example of "behind the Sun": Sun in Gemini, Venus in Aries or Taurus. The Venusian Dilemma of Venus behind the Sun can arise when someone loves their beloved with all they've got but still falls short of the beloved's expectations or their needs for a specific kind of love. This person can also be slower to fall in love, as if needing more time for the experience of love to reach their very being (Sun).

Those with the Venusian Dilemma of Sun conjunct Venus may first have to realize a higher level of self-acceptance and self-love before feeling ready to share their love with another. When Venus is in the same sign as the Sun, the affectionate nature can be embodied as charm, charisma, grace and animal magnetism. This becomes more evident with tighter Sun/Venus conjunctions. This conjunction can represent the experience of *being the love that you seek*.

When Venus is ahead of the Sun by one or two signs, affections may be quicker to rise into expression. The dilemma for such a person and for their beloved can occur if the former expects the latter to match their own *quick to affection* responses. Those with Venus ahead of the Sun may fall quicker in love and maybe faster than the beloved can reciprocate; frustrations and misunderstandings ensue.

Overall, the Venusian Dilemma testifies to how each person can know and experience love differently and with its own distinct sense of timing and expression. It can also show how love can deepen and mature as differences are accepted, embraced and celebrated between friends, lovers and others.

The Guiding Planet and the Dispositor Planet to the North Node

The Guiding Planet

Like all the techniques introduced here, this simple but possibly profound method needs to be tested, preferably with one's own chart first before applying it to the charts of others. The "guiding planet" refers to the first planet (or planets, if conjunct) behind the Sun that does not share the Sun's sign; one sign back.

For example, in my chart Neptune in Libra is the first planet behind my Scorpio Sun that doesn't share the Sun's sign. Neptune is my *guiding planet*. Looking back over my entire life since childhood, it's clear how much I have been guided by my dreams—the Muse of Neptune. Since Neptune closely conjuncts my Saturn in Libra, it has never been enough for me to just dream without finding ways to give them form and make my dreams come true. This has turned me into a *reality-based dreamer*.

My wife Sylvi has a Gemini Sun with Venus in Aries as the first planet behind her Sun and not in the same sign. *She's guided by Venus*. Sylvi tells me that she's been guided by her sense of beauty, art, status and aesthetics for as long as she can remember. The Guiding Planet theory can have profound implications given its role as a dependable principle of meaningful guidance and life direction. But this method deserves to be tested many times over to substantiate its claims. As a guiding principle, this method does not compete with the North Node as a guiding light, but augments it.

Examples: With her 10th house North Node, Sylvi's visual art has been displayed in European and USA art galleries and her music is heard all around the world. My 3rd house North Node has been augmented by Neptune's guidance, inspiring the many screenplays I've written for the films I've produced.

The Dispositor Planet to the North Node

For some of us, the North Node area can feel beyond reach. Perhaps we have succumbed to inertia and feel stuck in the comfort zone of our South Node area. One way to energize the North Node sign is by locating its "dispositor planet," and engaging that force through experiences related to its house placement. Each astrological sign is associated with its own resident planet, or force, that takes on the role of its "dispositor planet."

Dispositor planets for each sign are:

ARIES (Mars)
TAURUS and LIBRA (Venus)
GEMINI and VIRGO (Mercury)
CANCER (Moon)
LEO (Sun)
SCORPIO (Pluto)
SAGITTARIUS (Jupiter)
CAPRICORN (Saturn)
AQUARIUS (Uranus)
PISCES (Neptune)

Here's how it works. Say your North Node is in Sagittarius in the 11th Community State with its dispositor planet Jupiter residing in your 2nd House. To energize this Sagittarius North Node, you'd start by engaging in experiences that increase your sense of self-worth. These experiences can activate *the expansive force of Jupiter* sending resonant frequencies received by Sagittarius. Strengthening the sense of inner value then supports social confidence.

Another example: Let's say Aries North Node is in the 5th Creative State with its dispositor planet Mars residing in the 1st State of Being. Energizing this creative Aries North Node may require more experience with self-motivation, of starting yourself up, not waiting for anyone to get you going. Self-starting experiences can activate *the visceral force of Mars* sending resonant frequencies received by Aries, strengthening personal drive to support the courage to create.

As with the other methods presented here, applying the Dispositor Planet technique requires practice and commitment to the field of actual experience. This cannot always occur sitting in front of a computer screen or reading a book. You may have to actually get up and get out of the house to have the experience. Otherwise, astrology can become just another mind game where the belief that something is happening remains disconnected from actual experience.

Grand Trines and Grand Crosses
Constellations of Consequence, Part One

NOTE: When calculating Grand Trines and Grand Crosses, I don't include the Nodal Axis or Asteroids. The Moon's Nodes are orientation points, not planets, and unless an Asteroid conjuncts a planet, I don't believe it has the holding power essential for keeping a Grand Cross or a Grand Trine together.

The Grand Trine

Grand trines are somewhat rare in charts and can sometimes indicate uncommon talents in those inclined to artistic, musical, literary and theatrical expression. These triangulating geometries can make life very easy as well as very difficult for these individuals. There can be a kind of fortuitousness and good luck in how they move through life, as if watched over by guardian angels. This same sense of good fortune can also encourage a sense of entitlement and expectation for others to recognize, or worship, their exalted fates; the more enlightened a person, the less entitlement they exhibit. As with planets or combinations of planets, the integration of their forces plays a key role in the extent these Grand Trines can be consciously worked with or whether they simply continue trining on their own.

Grand Earth Trines

When three planets are in different Earth signs (Taurus, Virgo, Capricorn) and each planet is within a 4-degree orb of trining each other (120 degrees, approximately), a Grand Earth Trine is formed. Grand Earth Trines represent a grounded force of grace on the material plane, supporting great harmony from intention into manifestation. Earth magic.

Grand Water Trines

When three planets are in different Water signs (Cancer, Scorpio, Pisces) and each planet is within a 4-degree orb of trining each other, a Grand Water Trine is formed. A Grand Water Trine represents a fluid force of grace on the spiritual plane, and supports great harmony within the dimension of feeling. Water magic. (Refer to Kurt Cobain's chart in the "Six Major Aspects" section.)

Grand Air Trines

When three planets are in different Air signs (Gemini, Libra, Aquarius) and each planet is within a 4-degree orb of trining each other, a Grand Air Trine is born. This Grand Trine represents a force of accelerating grace at the level of mind. Swiftness of thought and rapid assimilation of information finds harmony with articulation of ideas and connecting with others. Air magic.

Grand Fire Trines

When three planets are in different Fire signs (Aries, Leo, Sagittarius) and each planet is within a 4-degree orb of trining each other, a Grand Fire Trine is formed. A Grand Fire Trine represents a strong creative force of grace through the dimension of intuition. Creativity flows in spontaneous flights of perpetual inspiration. Fire magic.

The Grand Cross

Grand Cross configurations are more rare than Grand Trines, and represent an altogether different dynamic. Whereas Grand Trines represent powerful harmonies, a Grand Cross articulates a high-powered tension of four squares bound together in a cruciform by two oppositions. Though everyone has their own cross to bear, those born under the sign of a Grand Cross may sense or feel it more than others. There can be a premonitory sense of having a special destiny accompanied by a guilt complex or feelings of inadequacy to be able to fulfill the life purpose they believe they are here for.

Due to the multiple square aspects, these individuals can be high-powered and productive, or they can appear withdrawn and caved in on themselves, depending on whether or not the ever-mounting inner tensions within their Grand Cross are finding release. Square aspects symbolize tension, and without outlets for their expression, mounting pressures can implode into a kind of caving in effect. As with any planets or combinations of planets, the integration of forces plays a key role in the degree these Grand Crosses can be consciously worked with or whether they continue unconsciously on their own.

Grand Cardinal Cross

A Grand Cardinal Cross engages four planets in different cardinal signs (Aries, Cancer, Libra, Capricorn) sharing squares and oppositions all within a 6-degree orb. The cardinal mode infuses the Grand Cardinal Cross with an outgoing, combustive energy pushing to manifest accomplishments. Goals, aspirations, and ambitions have only to be clarified as the power to bring them to fruition already exists. When activated, this Grand Cross can transmit a powerful outgoing force of productivity.

Grand Mutable Cross

A Grand Mutable Cross engages four planets in different mutable signs (Gemini, Virgo, Sagittarius, Pisces) sharing squares and oppositions within a 6-degree orb. The mutable mode infuses a highly interactive agency that feeds on external stimulation to sustain itself. When sustained, the Grand Mutable Cross transmits a powerful mobilizing influence for energizing others and accelerating their momentum.

Grand Fixed Cross

A Grand Fixed Cross engages four planets in different fixed signs (Taurus, Leo, Scorpio, Aquarius) sharing squares or oppositions within a 6-degree orb. The fixed modality represents a potent concentration of forces that, more than the other crosses, amplifies the mystery of the crucifixion archetype *in the body*. Not just another Bible story, the crucifixion represents the crux of a surrendered life and the potential for self-transcendence. When realized, the Grand Fixed Cross concentrates consciousness within a spiritual capacity for sacrificing the self to greater powers and causes.

T-Squares and Yods
Constellations of Consequence, Part Two

NOTE: When calculating T-square and Yods, I do not include the Nodal Axis or the Asteroids. The Moon's Nodes are orientation points, not planets, and unless an Asteroid conjuncts a planet, I don't believe it has the staying power to sustain the tensions of a T-square or the wobbly double quincunx of a Yod.

T-Squares

This configuration is made up of an opposition between two planets (either planet can also conjunct others) and a third planet (which also can be conjunct others) that squares both sides of the opposing points. Finding a T-square in a horoscope is not a rare sighting. Though two T-squares are rare, three T-squares are almost unheard of (though they do happen).

Much like a negative/positive charged battery, the opposing planets generate energy between themselves. The third point, the squared planet, absorbs and accumulates the pressures of the energies oscillating between the opposing points. The whole T-square represents a kind of energy-generating engine within the psyche- building internal pressures that seek release into a specific target zone. The tensions of a T-square find release in the opposite house of the pressure accumulator planet, the target zone.

There's a T-square in my natal chart (refer to the first page of the "12 Symbolic Sets" section). Mars and Uranus share an opposition and both these planets square the accumulator point of 11th house Saturn/Neptune in Libra. The release point of this T-square is into the 5th house, the Creative State. The ongoing pressures of this T-square find release as long as I can find ways to *stay creative*. If I don't abide by this guideline, I start experiencing uncomfortable social pressures and disappointments (11th house Saturn/ Neptune), and my role in the community starts imploding. With my 3rd house North Node in Aquarius (part of the 11th house, Uranus, Aquarius set), my sense of purpose is also involved and energized by this T-square as long as I abide by 5th house creative agendas. (Refer also to the chart of Venus Williams in the "Six Major Aspects" section.)

The Yod

Yod is Hebrew for "Hand of God" or "Finger of Fate" and links with The Hermit card in the Tarot. Astrologically, a Yod refers to an exotic configuration of three planets. Two of them share a sextile aspect as the *legs of the Yod*. A third planet, *the Yod head*, shares a 150-degree quincunx aspect with each leg. Yods can be tricky to interpret since both quincunx angles from the Yod head to each leg have different functions: one quincunx point *catalyzes* and the other is *catalyzed*. (Refer to "The Quincunx" in the "Six Major Aspects" section.)

Yods are genuinely mysterious to me. I honestly don't know why or how they work the way they do. As with most everything I know about astrology, what I know about Yods comes from reading over a thousand horoscopes and noting consistent patterns that arise. What I have seen so far with Yods is how they can symbolize dramatic experiences of how time and timing can be experienced as either benevolent or malevolent, as in good timing and bad timing.

I think everyone knows the difference between good and bad timing. Good timing means being at the right place at the right time; it feels fortuitous and lucky. Poor or bad timing can feel like missing the bus or being at the right place but at the wrong time or vice versa. Sometimes what appears as bad luck can become good luck in delay and sometimes what appears as good luck may not be so lucky in the long run. Time and timing can be slippery that way.

The key to working productively with Yods is about *integrating the Yod head* (its sign and house plus aspects to planets, especially conjunctions). The idea here is that the sense of timing improves as the Yod head becomes more integrated. Poor to bad timing can continue if the Yod head remains ignored and left to the winds, so

Experiential Astrology

to speak. The legs of the Yod (the sextiled planets) may also become stronger as their forces are integrated. Well-integrated Yods can represent a life lived within the magical dimension of synchronicity, the standard time zone of the Universe.

TRANSITS
Rites of Passage

Tracking the Timing of Change
Nodal Axis Returns, Transits from Jupiter, Saturn, Chiron, Uranus, Neptune and Pluto

I admit to not knowing exactly why or how the astrological technique of transits work. After studying and applying this method for over three decades, I'm still astonished by its accuracy to delineate *the timing of change*. I apply the method of tracking transits to measure the timing of life experiences, but *not the causes*. It's silly to blame Saturn for frustrations I experience after ignoring my own limitations; or to blame Pluto for my naiveté around impermanence, loss and death as natural cycles of life. I also don't use this method to predict the future. I think the best way to predict the future would be *to create it*. As with all my astrological interpretations, I perceive current and upcoming transits as *tendencies,* not absolutes.

The orbit of each planet marks a specific duration of time and timing. By studying transits as the timing of change, I can sometimes align my intentions, projects or schedules with that timing. I don't look at my transits every time I leave the house or when I make appointments. What fun is that? I look at my transits when I feel a change in the air, and when I'd like to know more about the *what, where and how* of these changes. Sometimes reading the transits are spot on, and sometimes they can be way off.

You will need an Ephemeris to track the transits. I recommend *The American Ephemeris for the 21st Century* by Neil F. Michelson and Rique Pottenger. This book lists the daily positions for each planet from the year 2000 to 2050. Online versions are also available for past centuries. Most astrology software also includes an Ephemeris. The astrology program I have been using for the past twenty years, and the one I recommend is "TimePassages" (available for PC and Mac).

Though tracking the transits of Sun, Moon, Mercury, Venus and Mars can sometimes prove useful, we will instead focus on Nodal Axis returns and the transits of Jupiter, Saturn, Chiron, Uranus,

Neptune and Pluto. In this "Transits" section, I will not present any formulaic lists of transits with all of the aspects to all of the planets, but instead focus on the nature and purpose of the distinct energies symbolized by the transiting planet. For more detailed descriptions on how transits aspect each and every planet, I refer you to Robert Hand's classic book, *Planets in Transit: Life Cycles for Living*.

NOTE: Always start by identifying which State the transiting planet is passing through. This simple point can be easily overlooked when transits are squaring or opposing natal planets, distracting attention away from where the transit is actually coming from.

Nodal Axis Returns

The Nodal Axis returns to its original natal position every nineteen years, marking a rite of passage at ages 19, 38, 57, 76, and so forth. This passage refers to the development and substantiation of the karmic circumstances around the interplay of fate and destiny. This includes experiences with one's calling and sense of purpose (North Node) and the strengths, talents and habit patterns inherited from past lives. What characterizes any nodal rite of passage can be a heightened sense of alignment or misalignment with our calling and sense of purpose, as well as reflections on past lives through past-life memory recall.

The first passage at 19 can involve an important break from past family identification towards establishing one's own path and identity. Crossing the threshold from the home nest into the world at large can be turbulent with the crosscurrents between what family wants and what the self wants. The second passage at 38 can coincide with a significant crisis of separation, either from the community or one's current lifestyle or a marriage or a business, towards reassessing one's future trajectory. This passage can also coincide with the Uranus opposition transit and its metaphor of *the crossroads* (introduced later in this "Transits" section), what some call "the mid-life crisis."

The third passage at 57 coincides with the second Saturn Return and can carry extra *gravitas* for starting to make a grander statement of identity, purpose and a declaration of personal destiny. The third passage can also have a kind of *teetering effect* between completing what was left unfinished, and starting what is yet to become the future. The fourth passage at 76 can be synchronized with a final release of attachment to past ambitions and social status towards reflection on life lived so far and the greater mystery that lies ahead.

Jupiter Transits

Jupiter orbits around the Sun every twelve years, spending approximately one year in each house as it passes through the horoscope. From the time of your birth, every 12 years marks a Jupiter Return, a rite of passage when a personal outlook and belief can be tested and maybe expanded to develop philosophy, ethics and a personal vision of truth. Every six years the Jupiter opposition can coincide with confrontations to test beliefs and assumptions. Though these confrontations originate within the self, they can dramatize externally as face-offs with others with diametrically opposing views.

Jupiter Returns

The 12-year cycle of Jupiter Returns occur as we turn 12, 24, 36, 48, 60, 72 and so on...and lasts about a year. The first Jupiter return at 12 years often involves identifying with the views of friends, social cliques, and collective trends. By the second return at 24, a new perspective may emerge for how one sees the world beyond groupthink and previous tribal mind identification. The third Jupiter return at 36 can see an acceleration of learning towards expanding one's viewpoint with new vistas of experience and knowledge.

With the fourth Jupiter return at 48, there can be a consolidation and establishment of one's worldview as one's own, and can indicate a period of teaching what one knows. The fifth Jupiter

Experiential Astrology

return at 60 can ignite the next acceleration of learning to expand consciousness and deepen conscience through the experiences of Jupiter's house. This can also indicate a time of teaching and mentorship. The sixth Jupiter return at 72 marks a harvest of whatever wisdom may have been earned and a clearer sense of what has mattered the most. This return and the following one at 84 may not be easy or comfortable given the choices made throughout life and how they shaped one's beliefs about self and the world. Some end up bitter, while others end serene.

Perceptual Shifts

Jupiter transits coincide with perceptual shifts and indicate where we may be ready to perceive more reality defined by the house Jupiter is transiting through. This expansive force symbolized by Jupiter can be experienced firsthand after investing more faith or belief in any situation symbolized by the state Jupiter is passing through. That's the idea. Jupiter passing through the 1st State of Being might be a good time to show more belief in yourself and your firsthand experiences. Jupiter passing through the 2nd State of Survival marks a good time to invest more belief in your values and your income-generating processes. Jupiter through the 3rd State of Mind calls for more faith in your ability to learn, communicate and make connections with others. And so on...

An Uplifting Expanse

When we perceive more reality in any given area (State), we can become more aware of what we actually care about and what we have no business caring about. Any expansion of consciousness, no matter how temporary, can clarify perspective around the context of what appears meaningful and what appears meaningless. When Jupiter's expansive force activates, we may feel a buoyant uplifting spirit where there may have previously been constriction, tunnel vision, or loss of humor. However, this same expansiveness can also spur excessive risk-taking, recklessness and over-extending yourself beyond your means. Jupiter the Exaggerator.

Saturn Transits

Saturn orbits around the Sun every 29 years while spending 2–3 years in each house as it goes. From birth, every 29 years marks a Saturn return, a rite of passage when reality structures are tested, demanding examination, correction and follow-through. Reality structures refer to the logistics of how time, space and existence are managed, or not. Often times, when these break down or have fractured, Foreman Saturn shows up in this area with her crew.

The Construction Crew

I like to look at Saturn transits through the houses as a construction crew surveying the area for fractures, leaks and whatever needs fixing to restore integrity there. If nothing needs fixing, the transit may pass without notice. If more serious problems exist in an area (the house), especially from past neglect and irresponsibility, there can be a sense of mounting pressure to finish what has been left undone or done poorly. Ignore the pressures and risk failure; do the work and know success. Saturn represents integrity as the capacity for follow-through to complete the tasks at hand.

Saturn Returns

Saturn Returns happen when we turn 29, 58, 87 and so on. During each passage, the Saturn return can occur once, twice or three times depending on how often Saturn goes retrograde and can last anywhere from a few months to two years. The two to three years following any Saturn return can often be a time for *following through* with whatever decisions and commitments were made during the Saturn return itself—*the post-Saturn Return integration zone.*

As the twenties come to an end, the first Saturn return takes hold between the ages of 28 and 30, marking a rite of passage into adulthood. Individuals obviously mature at differing rates, and what defines "adulthood" depends on personal experience or lack thereof. The first Saturn return is typically a time when pressures build around consolidating one's place in the real world: *What do you want to be when you grow up?*

This can be a time for facing failures, mistakes and errors in judgment if real world limitations—*of time, energy, skills, talents, money and other resources*—have been ignored. This can also be a time of great success, achievement and maturation as these limitations are recognized, accepted and worked with.

Though the nature of each Saturn return differs, each one can be characterized by the sign and house of natal Saturn (and aspects shared with planets or nodes). The first Saturn return can often pivot around whether to adhere to success and status defined by consensus mainstream standards or by the individual. Many are well-suited for success on society's terms, and happily conform with little argument. Some who achieve success in this way can live fulfilling lives, while others who follow the same course end up miserable. If you cannot agree on society's terms, look to your natal Saturn to find the kind of success and status that can be achieved *on your own terms* after they are defined and aligned with. (Refer to *Saturn, A Compressive Force of Commitment* in the "12 Symbolic Sets" section.)

Reality Checks

Reality structures are tested during Saturn squares (every seven years) and oppositions (every fourteen years, which can coincide with experiences of conflicts (squares) and confrontations (oppositions) with the self and others around issues of integrity, status and responsibility. Generally speaking, Saturn transits coincide with integrity tests to our ability, or inability, to manifest our intentions in real time.

When Saturn transits coincide with a greater frequency of mistakes, errors in judgment, frustration and failure, it usually means a naïveté or negligence of existing limitations around the logistics of *time* (schedules), *space* (territory and boundaries), and *knowledge* (know-how). When conflicts and confrontations (squares and oppositions) start with an oblivion of one's own limitations, they dramatize outwardly as face-offs with others asserting conflicting and/or diametrically opposed versions of the issues at hand.

Saturn issues include *success, failure, authority, fears, responsibility, integrity* and *status*. When transiting Saturn squares and opposes natal planets, it's usually a good time to slow down and take stock of the situations at hand defined by the houses involved and any planets aspected by the transit.

Decisions and Boundaries

Saturn transits can coincide with a pressure to make an important decision, made significant by its potentially long-term consequences. Once the limitations of the given situation (house, sign, aspects) can be exposed, recognized and accepted, they can help clarify and support more *reality-based* decision making. Those previously inclined to indecisiveness may obviously find these Saturn transits more challenging, while also providing an opportunity to become more accountable for their lives.

Saturn transits can parallel a time of testing personal boundaries in the state it's visiting, and any natal planets Saturn may be aspecting. This can involve boundaries within the self, in relationships, at work, or with family members. Boundary work amounts to knowing when and where to draw a line to make your limitations known to yourself and whomever else it may involve. This could be limitations of personal energy, your money, your time, and anything else that needs conserving. During Saturn transits, the sense of time itself can feel as if it's *slowing down to a dead standstill*—perhaps Saturn's way of getting your attention...

The Force of Commitment

As the constrictive force of Saturn passes through a house, it can be a time to commit more fully to whatever issues are innate to that state (also, planets aspected by the transit). Saturn through the 1st house demands more commitment to firsthand experiences as a source of authority; *self-commitment*. Saturn through the 2nd house may require a closer examination of core values and personal finances to determine whether any restructuring of these issues is necessary. Saturn through the 3rd house can coincide with the pressure to buckle down and commit to your education and improve communication skills. And so forth...

Maturation

The timing of Saturn transits parallels an internal process of crystallization through *maturation and aging*. Saturn transits can occur when our most cherished ideals and expectations are confronted and distorted by reality, the existing conditions of our lives. These tough "character building" transits mark a time for reality-checking ungrounded assumptions about what can and cannot be achieved, given real life limitations and inadequacies at hand. If these limits are denied, failures and mistakes may continue in the house Saturn is passing through. *Saturn is your friend.* Accept your shortcomings; embody your humanity. By accepting your flaws, you may become ready to accept the flaws of others and the endless shortcomings of an imperfect world. Saturn transits mark a growing up time.

Chiron Transits

Chiron takes about 52 years to circle the Sun. This means that anyone who lives to 52 will experience their first, and possibly only, *Chiron return*. Since Chiron's orbit is highly elliptical, the period of the first Chiron square deviates from person to person. Though mine occurred between the years of 15 and 18, it may not occur to others until much earlier or later. The same goes for the Chiron opposition and other aspects made by transiting Chiron. With that said, each Chiron transit brings new insights into the internal dynamics symbolized by natal Chiron.

The square aspect can expose a conflict between Chiron's natal state and the state transiting Chiron is passing through. The opposition can indicate confrontational Chirotic issues—such as rebelling against authority figures—until the issue can be traced back to its source through *self-confrontation*. The 52-year Chiron return marks *a time of reckoning* to discover whether we're going to continue sabotaging ourselves for the rest of our lives as victims, or whether we're ready to start acting as a force of conscious subversion (in Chiron's state). Chiron says, *"Subvert or be subverted."*

Wounds and Injuries

With Chiron orbiting between Saturn and Uranus, its transits can coincide with literal physical wounds or health issues linked with the skeletal (Saturn) and/or the nervous systems (Uranus). Though these woundings can happen anytime, I've seen them occur more frequently during the Chiron opposition at 26 and the Chiron return at 52.

If physical injury or pains arise during these transits, it's a good time to examine how they may have originated as a self-inflicted wound, either done on purpose, accidentally or unconsciously. To determine the cause, examine natal Chiron against your life situation to ascertain the extent you may be trying too hard to conform to consensus reality standards and values in Chiron's house. If you have, you may better understand your pattern of self-sabotage (in the unintegrated Chiron), and it may be time to start acting more as a conscious force of subversion in that area. (Refer to *Comet Chiron* in the "Theory and Praxis" section.)

Transpersonal Transits
Uranus, Neptune, Pluto as Outside Shocks

Transits from the outer planets—*Uranus, Neptune and Pluto*—represent the timing and synchronicity of evolutionary triggers from transpersonal experiences originating beyond the control—and often, beyond the comprehension—of ego. These experiences correspond to the awakening of sovereignty (Uranus); deepening empathy and compassion (Neptune); and ego-death, rebirth and spiritual empowerment (Pluto).

These three transpersonal agencies can be experienced by the ego-personality as three types of *outside shock,* each delivering a kind of one-two punch: *one to the sleeping ego* and *one to the awakening soul.* Inside shocks are self-created; some people are masters at shocking themselves silly. Outside shocks arrive from beyond the ego. Ego is defined here as *self-image* and *the emotional investment sustaining any self-image.* Soul is not defined here beyond an ineffable presence capable of experience.

Uranus transits correspond to shocks of *oppression and freedom*; Neptune, shocks of *isolation and unity*; Pluto, shocks of *impermanence, death and rebirth.* Do the planets shock us? No, of course not. I do think we may unwittingly attract outside shocks into our lives to the extent we are still naive to, or in denial of, the objective truths of *Uncertainty* (Uranus), *Indivisibility* (Neptune), and *Impermanence* (Pluto). These transits can be synchronized with an awakening to oppression (Uranus), the breakdown of psychological defenses obscuring the unity of life (Neptune), and an exposure to the stupefying stagnation of a dead-end existence (Pluto). Shocks arrive as fate. How we respond to shock determines our destiny.

Uranus Transits

Uranus makes a full orbit around the Sun, and around each chart, every 84 years; the first and last Uranus Return occurs at age 84. Between the ages of 39 and 42, the Uranus opposition marks a rite of passage that can feel like arriving at a *crossroads.* Whatever life path has been taken now arrives at a fork in the road with two or more different directions to consider before moving ahead. This transit can be characterized by *a significant pause* to reflect on whether or not there's some experience that's been missed out on as a result of taking the course up to this juncture.

In traditional terms, this rite of passage is called the "mid-life crisis." Standing at the crossroad, if you realize that your freedom has been seriously compromised *by the choices made to get where you are,* you may jump track and chase down whatever experience you believe can restore your autonomy. (Examples: The CEO who suddenly quits his successful Wall Street firm to set sail around the world. The professor who leaves his university tenure to live in an Israeli Kibbutz.) Unexpectedly jumping track like this can appear insane to anyone thinking they know you based solely on the life you were living. If, upon reviewing your life, you realize that your freedom has not been compromised, congratulations. Your life can now move forward into a new era of blossoming, and a harvesting of your dreams and ambitions.

Textbook astrology calls Uranus "the freedom planet," yet very few books explain what is actually meant by "freedom." Though the desire for freedom burns brightest in the hearts of slaves and prisoners, almost everyone in society can be trapped in their own kind of cage. Those who are unaware, or in denial, of any oppression can still believe they are free. This very naïveté may explain why any sudden awareness of a previously unknown oppression can feel shocking. This shock of oppression can trigger disruptive reactions and knee-jerk reflexes of revolt against the perceived oppressor.

Though anger can vitalize action, true freedom requires precise knowledge of the actual source of oppression. Some oppression is self-imposed and some comes from lifelong cultural conditioning. It's important to know the difference. What has been self-imposed can also be self-eliminated. Cultural conditioning, family upbringing, and the codes of conduct inherited from ancestors can be more difficult to identify and bypass. True freedom here means freedom from oppression. Remove the block and innate freedom remains. We are born free and are more free than we realize due to the deep sleep and mass hypnosis of cultural and societal oppression. Yet it is also possible to wake up. But then what?!

The Shock of Freedom

True freedom can be shocking at first. How much freedom can you live with? Whatever house Uranus is transiting through refers to an area of our lives where we may be ready to awaken to more freedom. Uranus transits often coincide with "wake-up" calls to previously shrouded patterns of oppression, places where we have been fast asleep to our innate autonomy. However, before this freedom can be experienced we may have to first face any habits of oppression in that area (house). Whether these are self-imposed or inherited by schools, teachers, parents, religions or the books we've read, Uranus transits coincide with "wake-up" calls to where we may have been fast asleep to our innate autonomy.

For example, when Uranus transits the 3rd house, we may wake up to patterns of intellectual oppression embedded in how we use language: the ways we think, speak, write and interpret experiences. We might discover ways of talking that ring false, or we may be shocked at our inability to simply tell the truth, or shocked by finally being able to speak our truth without self-censoring. Once these oppressions are faced, we are ready for more freedom of speech and creative, or independent, thought.

Uncertainty vs. Anxiety

When the shock of Uranus transits wakes up the sleeping ego to the objective truth of Uncertainty, that truth can arouse anxiety. But uncertainty is not the same as anxiety. Uncertainty is a fact of life; anxiety expresses a *reaction* to this fact. Anxiety measures the threshold for how much uncertainty can be allowed before we start behaving like a nervous monkey.

Anxiety can be managed by learning to permit more uncertainty. By relaxing the compulsion to be so damn sure about anything, the state of uncertainty, of not knowing, opens the mind to new possibilities. By allowing more uncertainty, the mystery of each moment unfolds as *a creative state*. In any genuine state of uncertainty, nobody knows what will happen next—it's a fluid moment, full of potential, ready to be discovered and shaped into whatever we want. Creative response to the state of uncertainty makes artists of us all.

Acceleration

Transpersonal shocks that come with Uranus transits and those of Pluto and Neptune are neither positive nor negative but *neutral*. How we respond to shocks determines whether the experience turns negative and painful or positive and joyous. Transiting Uranus can signify unexpected accelerations in those areas corresponding to the house Uranus is passing through, and planets being aspected by the transit.

When Uranus conjuncts Venus, relationships can jump on the fast track. We discover how free or smothered we are. The degree of disruption and chaos that ensues during Uranus-to-Venus transits can be a measure of how oppressive or liberating relationships have become. The greater the oppression, the greater the disruption that follows when Uranus transits any of the personal forces.

Experimentation

Uranus transits can arrive when we are ready for more experimentation in the house it's passing through. We might experience a second chance to reinvent ourselves in an area previously over-regimented by too much structure, obsolete habit patterns, or tyranny—our own or someone else's. Uranus transits are synchronized with a destabilizing influence in areas that may have grown too rigid. These transits can be upsetting, but they can also be exhilarating with fresh ideas and visions. When obsolete routines and redundant habits wobble and careen, a new freedom emerges to reinvent ourselves through the chaos.

Intelligence Increase

Impersonal species stupidity (not personal stupidity) may be the greatest cause of human oppression and suffering on Earth. Once awakened to this dreadful enlightenment, we can either wise up or remain part of the problem. Uranus transits don't automatically increase intelligence. They can, however, expose an evolutionary imperative to increase intelligence.

Defined in Uranian terms, intelligence includes many functions including Intellect such as Imagination, Intuition, Body wisdom, Emotional and Social intelligence, Inspiration and Dreams. As the higher octave of Mercury, the mundane intellect, Uranus transits can coincide with an expanded experience of intelligence through an awakening to uncertainty as a creative state. (Refer to my book, *The Eight-Circuit Brain: Navigational Strategies for the Energetic Body*, The Original Falcon Press.)

Neptune Transits

Neptune makes a full orbit around the Sun and around each chart every 165 years. At the most basic level of existence, we are made from the stuff of stars. It is easy to overlook the underlying unity of all life when so many differing ideas and beliefs divide people from each other and sustain the illusion of separateness. When these illusions are taken too seriously, they crystallize into *an illusion of reality*. When this self-delusion reaches critical mass, it may attract Neptunian shocks overwhelming the separatist ego with *the undeniable objective truth of indivisibility*. We may have a God experience, a Goddess or Divinity experience. It doesn't matter what's it's called; what matters is the direct, all-encompassing experience of oneness with all of Life. Astrology calls this Neptune.

Boundary Loss and Sacrifice

Neptune transits can herald anywhere from a two to five year era of slow-motion boundary loss in a gradual dissolution of defenses, assumptions and expectations obscuring the unifying experience of indivisibility. These more gentle shocks come in waves, like the ocean that mythological Neptune (aka Poseidon), governs. When personal expectations have become overly inflated, Neptune transits befuddle the separatist ego with disappointment, disillusionment and heartbreak.

Neptune transits can also bring on waves of mercy, compassion and inspiration for those ready to open up to the cosmos. It's what mysticism is all about: *opening up to the cosmos.* Neptune transits can expose an emerging transpersonal need for restoring a lost sense of the sacred in our lives, and what has divided us from the spiritual. During these transits, we can experience sacrifices necessary for restoring the lost sense of the sacred. In this way, these transits can work in tandem with natal asteroid Vesta in this opening to the sacred.

When self-imposed and culturally-conditioned barriers cause suffering through their illusion of separateness, the brittle ego is more easily shocked by the objective unity of life itself. Neptune transits can bring about a blurring of personal boundaries in the areas (houses and aspected planets) where fixations and prejudices have been sustaining arbitrary separations from our inner lives, from others and from nature itself. Like the political borders dividing one country from the next, it's easy to lose track of the one planet and the one human race we are all part of.

Brain Fog

Neptune transits can parallel a time when we experience a kind of fog effect in our heads, creating mental confusion and disorientation. This kind of brain fog expresses the Neptune effect of dissolving obsolete divisions in the psyche through bewilderment. Like a ship adrift in a massive fog bank, Neptune transits may bring experiences of "zero visibility"—a loss of perspective to understand what might be happening. Ships navigating fog banks depend on sonar to avoid shipwreck. Navigating through the fog bank of Neptune transits requires the sonar of intuition and the somatic compass of our five senses. This fog expresses nondual consciousness; it's of one piece! Neptune's fog bank confounds intellectual capacity for comparison, analysis and deductive attempts to explain it. It cannot be explained, but it can be experienced. Intuition and the somatic compass of *the five senses* allow us to surf the waves of Neptune without having to understand it.

The Illusion of Reality

The timing of Neptune transits can also inspire ineffable beauty and idyllic experiences in both the house it's passing through and natal planets aspected by this transit. These transits can bring a gentling influence, taking the edge off of otherwise harsh situations. They can just as often incite self-delusion when precious illusions are mistaken for reality—the mirage in the desert, the dream lover who turns out to be a jerk, the ideal business venture that goes bankrupt. These disillusionments can evolve us if we can live with less illusion about ourselves, each other, and the world.

Neptune transits can attune us to higher frequencies of pure potential within us through the oceanic consciousness of all-inclusive, all-enveloping awareness. As ocean waves crash on the beach shaping and dissolve the borders of the shoreline, so do our own boundaries shift, disappear and reappear again, transformed. Neptune represents the higher octave of Venus' evolving personal love towards universal compassion.

Pluto Transits

Pluto makes a full orbit around the Sun and around each chart every 248 years. When the transit of Pluto conjuncts, squares, trines or opposes a personal planet, it's usually a once in a lifetime event. Pluto transits seem highly synchronized to expose a specific area where something has ended or may be about to end. There can be an interim zone between any real ending and a new beginning, a kind of *bardo* zone where nothing seems to be happening ("bardo" is a Tibetan Buddhist term for a disembodied interim between incarnations).

This idea of the *bardo* is also mirrored in waking life where it can be characterized by an overall sense of *drift*, like a boat unanchored and without a rudder. In this aimless drifting phase nothing seems to be happening. That's because the real action is occurring beneath the surface of awareness where Plutonic forces work their alchemy. One day nothing happens and the next day, everything changes.

A Multiplicity of Stages

Pluto transits can last anywhere from two to five years and sometimes longer. In this time period, many stages of transformation can unfold, reflected by the multiple totems assigned to Pluto, Scorpio and the 8th house: *the scorpion, the spider, the serpent, the vulture, the eagle, the dove, the Phoenix*. Pluto transits expose many types of death, some of which can manifest literally as physical death, either one's own or the death of loved ones. More often than not, Pluto transits manifest in far less literal ways, such as the death of a belief system (9th house), death of a career (10th house), or the death of a marriage (7th house).

Death and dying processes also take on far more common forms such as inertia, stagnation, corruption, decay and degeneration. As an archetype, Pluto does not represent death *as a finality*, but as a metamorphosis of many phases, eventually leading to rebirth, resurrection, reincarnation. However, rebirth is not always guaranteed in the current life. Sometimes, suicide or other unexpected interruptions can postpone the current metamorphosis to pick up again in the next lifetime.

Exposure of Oneself to Oneself

During some Pluto transits there can be a disconcerting sense of exposure of oneself to oneself. It can feel a bit like walking through an X-ray, as if you are seeing through yourself and maybe seeing through the lies of society. This sense of transparency brings with it an exposure of where you may have been living a lie. It's as if the Pluto archetype simply wants those who are in its transit zone to become more honest, more true to their essential selves.

As we become more honest with ourselves and each other during and after Pluto transits, we may become a bit more *plutonic* ourselves. Seeing through the lies of others, we may feel compelled to confront them on their dishonesty—whether they are ready for it or not. I have noticed that this happen more often during Pluto transits that conjunct or oppose the Sun, ASC, Moon, Mercury, Mars or Venus.

Not everyone goes through the same Pluto transits at the same time. Those who do undergo Pluto transits can sometimes assume that others are sharing their experience. I think this projection can be traced back to how the transpersonal influence of Pluto transits links the personal ego with collective experience. Yes, we are all going to die but do you really have to shout it out on the rooftops? A lot of people still need their sleep and are not ready to wake up.

The Shock of Impermanence

In any exposure to death, whether it's death of a person or a dream or a relationship, we discover the objective truth of Impermanence; nothing lasts forever. Whether it's the death of old feelings or beliefs or a friendship or our reputation or the actual physical passing of someone dear to us, the shock of Impermanence devastates the naive ego's illusions of control and permanence. When we are attached to what or who has died (or is dying), our clinging creates its own suffering. The longer we cling, the longer the suffering lasts. Letting go of attachment to what has died or is dying transforms this suffering into healing.

Those living overly sheltered lives can naturally remain naive to the universal truth of Impermanence. Though the processes of death exist everywhere, unless you live in a war zone or in extreme squalor, most of these processes remain hidden in hospitals, prisons and hospices. When Pluto enters a house by transit and aspects natal planets, we may be exposed to something that is dying or has already died. The objective truth of Impermanence comes as the central shock of Pluto transits and is only "shocking" to the degree of ego naïveté; some people still insist they live forever. When wising up to Impermanence as an ongoing awareness, a deepening gratitude is born for the preciousness of every living moment.

Power Loss

In the face of any death during Pluto transits, there may be a feeling of fate, an unstoppable sense of inevitability. Whether it's the death of a romance or a job or the end of a friendship, feelings of helplessness can often accompany an actual ending. Helpless feelings are a natural response to losing control of a situation that was never under our control in the first place. *Feelings* of helplessness are not the same as *actually* being helpless, though it may *feel* that way at the time. There's always a choice when facing any real ending: to either keep holding on or to let go. If you hold on, you experience power loss. If you let go, power can be restored through the open space created by the release of attachment.

Empowerment

The underlying evolutionary imperative of all Pluto transits seems to be *empowerment,* though this power must be earned through enduring adversity, facing death, and letting go. By aligning with this empowerment process, we are more likely to face any difficulty head-on and triumph. However, this is no victory for ego but *for the soul.* Pluto transits often expose the futility of self-centered behavior, resulting in the defeat of ego. Sometimes, during an outright ego-death, our previously cherished self-concepts disintegrate and we are left clueless about who we are or who we are becoming.

Like a snake molting old skin, we grow by outgrowing obsolete versions of ourselves and emerge stronger, wiser and more powerful than before. We become a bit more plutonic ourselves. Pluto represents the higher octave of Mars, the force of our personal will, and the choice to align with the will of the cosmos itself; *not my will, but Thy Will.*

In Review: Human Shock Absorbers

Outer planet transits can sometimes arouse anxiety and fear which can be natural responses to any sudden influx of energies bigger than the ego and bigger than our bodies. In hard-hitting transits, such as Pluto crossing the natal Ascendant or conjunct the Moon, it can feel as if our very bodies and personalities are incapable of containing the transformative forces coursing through us; we may freak out and believe we are literally dying. Transpersonal energies are bigger than our personality, and require a larger body or vessel, such as a transpersonal cause, to circulate the power.

Transpersonal means *beyond* the ego but also *inclusive of* the ego. Worldwide suffering and nonstop tragedies have birthed countless transpersonal causes: the Peace Corps, the Red Cross, homeless shelters, Greenpeace, suicide hotlines, free food distribution, and so on. These larger bodies of transpersonal causes can act as media to circulate the big energies activated during transits from Uranus, Neptune and Pluto.

Those who have served a transpersonal cause often experience the sense of becoming as vessels for powerful collective currents of awakening (Uranus), compassion (Neptune), and transformation (Pluto). As we absorb and integrate these shocks, we can become as *human shock absorbers* capable of transmitting shocks to those who need them. As we are initiated to greater realities, so we become as initiators of these experiences for others, sometimes without realizing as much. The catalyzed become the catalysts.

PLANETARY FORCES AS SEXUAL REALITIES
The Complex Playing Fields of Sexuality

Part One:
Sun, Moon, Mercury, Venus, Mars

It seems odd how astrology and astrologers alike tend to shy away from discussing sex. Maybe this stems from confusion stirred up by so many cultural misrepresentations of the wild spectrum of human sexual response. For example, common labels for sexual orientations—*Heterosexual, Bisexual, Homosexual, Pansexual, Asexual, Transsexual, Omnisexual, etc.*—don't just refer to sexual realities but also to political ones.

Though I doubt astrology can actually discern gender or sexual orientation, I can imagine the planetary symbols as *sexual realities* regardless of gender, sexual tribe, or orientation. All of the planets including Sun and Moon will be introduced here as various forces of sexual complexity within the larger mystery and diversity of human sexual response. In Part One, we'll visit the Sun, Moon, Mercury, Venus and Mars. Part Two ventures into Jupiter, Saturn, Chiron, Uranus, Neptune and Pluto. Part Three explores the author's life-changing experience with a mysterious woman during a Pluto transit.

The Sun

Solar sex ignites the being. What is "the being"? It is not the understanding of it or any idea about it, but rather the subjective experience of inhabiting space and time as an entity. How can anyone know the being? By the experience of being enough, and by the presence of this "being enough" after we are affirmed for who we are—beyond what we do or are known for. The Sun is a star, and potentially so are beings—unless their light has been buried beneath the heavy sediment of societal, familial and cultural baggage. Solar sex arouses the being into becoming more of itself.

Astrologically speaking, when the being is confirmed, the Sun sign is turned on. Solar sex rarely leaves anyone feeling insignificant or diminished. Solar sex amplifies the being by enhancing the sense of selfhood. Like the Sun itself, when the being is turned on there's a greater emanation of luminosity and warmth. Astrologically, this can happen when certain forces (like the Moon, Venus, Jupiter or Neptune) in a lover's chart conjunct or oppose one's natal Sun.

The Solar-Lunar Couple

If the being yearns to expose more of itself, solar sex can arouse the uninhibited thrills of exhibitionism. In more conservative relationship structures, one lover may play out the Sun to the other's Moon—the more lunar person reflects, and revolves around, the more solar partner. Some lovers prefer the lunar function, just as others are happier being the only star in the room. Everybody is a star in potential. To become a star means to self-realize, and solar sex enhances self-realization. The courtship and romance of two self-realizing individuals, or stars, can revolve around a third mutual point of gravity, such as joint business ventures or shared creative projects. These "third point projects" initiate and sustain an interstellar polarity of binary stars in dynamic rapport at the level of being; *a rare and beautiful thing.*

Interstellar Passions

Marriages between stellar polarities can be challenging to maintain due to the escalation of luminosity and heat between two stars. And yet, more and more self-realizing stars are finding each other and refusing to settle for old-world, conventionally defined marriages. Stellar polarities have their own problems. The tempestuous interstellar marriage between Richard Burton (Scorpio Sun) and Elizabeth Taylor (Pisces Sun) played out their high solar drama in public and onscreen (Mike Nichol's film, *Who's Afraid of Virginia Woolf?*), generating torrents of heat, light and grand passion in splendorous explosions of chaos and devastation.

Today's Star is Tomorrow's Black Hole

The dark side of Sun-love acts out as the ego-based sexuality of escalating narcissistic hedonism. In extreme instances, this can shift towards unbridled personality worship with cult figureheads. Whether it's self-worship, worship from another, or adoration from the Many, ego inflation overemphasizes the individual Sun sign. Some cult leaders coax their devoted followers into multiple sex partners to maintain cult cohesion or to support the leader's immortality through baby-making. For centuries, traditional religious Gurus have attached themselves to colonies of sannyasins and disciples to circulate the dense accumulation of attention and power accrued through their exalted positions. Sexual scandals are a common downfall of many religious cults.

The Moon

When any sexual encounter leaves us feeling attached, the Moon was turned on. Not all sex is emotional, but when the Moon is involved, consider yourself bound. Emotions don't wait for your approval or comprehension to make their move. You become attached whether you want to or not. Emo-sex can fulfill unknown and unmet infantile needs for security and/or trust. Emotions have lives of their own, and act as powerful animistic forces not subject to the rules of intellect or moral judgment. Emotions can pass from one body to the next, making a home wherever they're needed.

Voodoo Love

Emotions dwell within your body until excited by another body showing profound receptivity to yours. Once excited, emotions can move to make a home in someone else and become part of their astral make up. Lovers appear in each other's dreams. Emotions act as spirits of animistic sex. If this sounds like voodoo love, emo-sex can feel like that. It puts you on pins and needles. If you're physically absent from somebody that your emotions have made a home in, you may find yourself irrationally longing for them when what you may really be missing are your own displaced emotions.

Karmic Sex

Emotional sex may be an unconscious attempt to bond with someone, regardless of whether they match any romantic ideal or image of the "perfect partner" or "dream lover." Sometimes the animal body feels a desperate need to make meaningful connection with someone—*anyone!*—to cope with a meaningless existence; attachment may not be wanted, but it may be necessary. With some emotional sex, an instant unexplainable familiarity with another arises. *"How can we know each other so deeply after only one night?"* Other times, a familial feeling arouses a small internal voice, *"This person could be my wife"* or *"This is my husband."* Perhaps deeper karmic contracts are at work. Have we returned from a past life to complete unfinished business? Check to see if South Nodes are aspected by each other's planets.

Emo-Sex Taboos

Sometimes lunar sex arouses taboo-ridden incestuous lust and sadomasochistic bondage rituals of dominance and submission (also see "Master/Slave Games" in "Part Two: Saturn"). Being tied up and physically immobilized in a safe climate can produce a profound sense of internal security to anyone with unmet infantile security needs. The Baby Man, the Baby Girl. Lunar sex can arouse a kind of familial romance with someone who feels like an emotional mother or father or big brother or little sister figure.

Incestuous love, not to be confused with literal incest, can also trigger feelings of guilt, annoyance, animosity, sibling rivalry, and tug-of-war power struggles to regain self-control if the relationship turns into an emotionally oppressive need structure. Power struggles can be fairly common to long-term emo-sex. Once exposed for the territorial surges they are, a healing of early sexual abuse or trauma can sometimes occur if there's enough emotional honesty expressed between those involved.

Bonds Between Lovers & Others

The need for emotional bonding through sex can be symbolized by natal lunar placements, the nadir, and 4th house planets. An Eighth house Moon, for example, may need emotional sex to arouse personal growth. Emotions surface in our most vulnerable states. To stay vulnerable with another, a shared sense of trust becomes essential. Deep bonds can also develop between lovers who are enduring an emotional nightmare together—*abortion, loss of a child, extramarital affairs, domestic violence, divorce, etc.*—and become much closer for it. Emotional bonds deepen between soldiers in battle amidst great adversity and danger, as do the silent pacts among police officers.

Mercury

When sexual encounters leave you chatty, talking to yourself, or chewing the ears off lovers who'll listen, Mercury has been turned on. Sometimes mental sex can indicate a need for more communication before being turned on. To whatever degree Mercury is involved, you're probably talking before sex, during sex, and after sex. To Mercury, communication and intelligence are aphrodisiacs. Watch for phone sex. Ambisexual Mercury, aka Hermes, travels between underworld and overworld without becoming residential to either. Fickle, oh yes. Hermes, the Puer Eterna, hops happily between bedrooms only to be gone next morning.

Ambisexual Hermes

Some astrologers and mythologists have naively associated Mercury with bisexuality, but I prefer the term "ambisexual", as one given to sexual ambivalence. Ambivalence is not a bisexual condition, but a human one. Ambivalence expresses a wavering signal of questionable excitement and complexity. This may be why Mercury and Hermes also symbolize the arts, intelligence and fickleness. Today, it's hot, and tomorrow, it's not. In its extreme, these

Mercurial influences can develop into the sexual indifference of asexuality.

The Idea of Sex

Astrological Mercury can represent ambivalence towards the physical sexual experience itself, leading to periods of celibacy or allegiance with the Asexual tribe. Sometimes, when Mercury is over-emphasized—*as in the Third House or in Gemini or Mercury conjunct the South node*—it can symbolize an all-talk-and-no-action attitude around sex. For some, the idea of sex becomes more arousing than the actual physical experience. This can often occur with the elderly, whose naturally waning physical energy and libido gives way to a new spectrum of lecherous fantasies, never meant to be fulfilled but savored nonetheless. Senex Sex.

Lovers talking all night about their personal problems can buffer sexual impulses with ambivalence. Talking can dampen excitement as a protective measure to inhibit lovers from having sex when they *only think they want it*. When there's no sexual heat, maybe it's better to play scrabble or read in bed or watch a movie.

Voyeurism

Astrological Mercury also symbolizes the intellectual capacity for witnessing our own actions and the actions of others. From a sexual perspective, this initiates voyeurism, a thrilling cocktail of safe physical distance and strong visual stimulus. When you are turned on by watching your partner enjoying sex with himself, herself or with another, voyeuristic passions are aroused. Heavy Mercury connections between lovers can also indicate shared voyeuristic fantasies. Talking about sexual fantasies, writing erotic stories together, and phone sex express the voyeurism of ambisexual Mercury.

Amoral Sex

Ambiguous sex may not require any commitment beyond the moment of being turned on, allowing more uncertainty to follow wherever excitement leads. Mercury sex can symbolize a kind of amoral sexuality unconcerned with right or wrong just so long as the sexual energy keeps moving and changing within the field of one's attention. Amoral sex pays little to no attention to consequences.

Venus

Falling in love can sometimes also have little to do with actually loving another person. Some, who are in love, can discover they don't actually like the other person. When two individuals are in love and sincerely like each other, there can be something miraculous. It is miraculous in any society charged up with instant gratification and advertisements of unrealistic romantic fantasies. Sometimes it can seem more like two fantasies falling in love than two persons.

The experience of love is not the same for everyone; love to one person can mean anything but love to another. When Venus is understood through all the twelve styles, it becomes more clear that there may be at least twelve ways to love. It's similar with Venus and aesthetics. Personal taste cannot be argued; you either like something or someone, or you don't. Love distinguishes itself.

When Love Defined Itself

The natal placement of Venus, its sign, and how it aspects other planets, can indicate how we have learned to be loved, and consequently, how we have come to define love for ourselves and those we love. The experience of love may have originated in how we were loved, or not, as children—what we had to do or how we had to behave before we were loved. *What were you loved for?* Look to the natal placement of Venus and aspects shared with other planets.

My natal 2nd House Venus in Sagittarius trining my 9th House Pluto reminds me how I was loved for being consistently big-hearted and positive when it came to family problems. Though the problems of a Finnish family freshly migrated to the western world were probably daunting, they never felt like a big deal to me. I have since felt loved for the understanding I bring others, both in my intimate partnerships and also through those who read my books. Sometimes I feel sad when I'm misunderstood by others until I realize how different love can be for everyone.

Sex with Friends

As sex blossoms from a ground of shared affinity, certain kinds of Venusian sex can feel like sex with friends; genuinely friendly sex also feels friendly after sex. Lovers can show great passion for each other (Mars!), yet without Venus, making love can burn quickly in the Martial fires of "fucking or fighting." To the Venus archetype, *love is everything.* In the face of cruelty, disillusionment, loss, bitterness, cynicism, hatred, fear, greed, envy, jealousy and the countless demons of human frustration, only love itself can accept and love how cruel, disillusioned, lost, cynical, egocentric, hateful, afraid, greedy and jealous we can be. Only love can dissolve negative emotion with heartfelt acceptance and compassion. Love is also vulnerable this way; it can be hurt, damaged and destroyed. Love needs tending to survive.

Love Needs Tending

On the Earth plane, Venus governs the vegetative kingdom—*flowers, fruit, vegetables, vines.* As with love, plants need tending to survive. Seeds dropped by birds or windblown across the land fall into fertile soil. Weather permitting, a seed sprouts and breaks ground to absorb the Sun's rays. Like any new love, vulnerable seedlings need care and protection or they can wither and die or be eaten by hungry deer. When love receives tender reminders, it offers itself more freely to those nurturing its unfolding blossoms and fruits.

Mars

Mars symbolizes the most purely visceral forms of sexual response. Martial sex vitalizes and motivates. You can't sit on this energy; something must be done with it. The Mars force responds to physical heat and reacts with excitement. As the Mars force increases within us, it can turn combustive and explosive: impulsive and spontaneous hot sex, power sex, angry sex, aggressive sex, combative and rough sex. In the extreme, Martial sex can turn into violent sex and rape which is no longer sex but the tyranny of psychopathic cruelty. These violent states can sometimes erupt with Pluto transits to Mars and sometimes with Pluto/Mars natal aspects.

Dangerous Sex

The accumulation of pent-up Mars force in incarcerated men finds release in masturbation, and sometimes, through the sexual violation of other men. In researching his book, *You Are Going To Prison* (Loompanics Press, 1994), Jim Hogshire discovered that twice as many men are raped inside American prison walls every year than are women raped on the outside. Predatory sexuality finds expression in the exaggerated Martial force of aggression. Some with a weaker Mars may feel aroused when a stronger Mars force acts on them. The weaker Mars person can sometimes jumpstart their own Mars through that osmosis. A weaker natal Mars may signify a greater desire to be motivated by external sources, just as a stronger natal Mars can be more self-driven. These tendencies can amplify with transits over natal Mars by conjunction, square or opposition from Saturn, Uranus, Neptune or Pluto.

Testosterone and the Sex Drive

The growth hormone testosterone exists in both men and women, yet the biological fact is testosterone exists in twice the amount in most men than in women. Researcher June Reinisch of Rutgers University discovered that increased testosterone levels in the body produce immediate aggression. Physiologist Julian Davidson performed a study on males with low sex drives. When given more testosterone, all showed an increase in sexual fantasy and desire. This resulted in the conclusion that testosterone is "the biological substrate of desire, at least in men." It makes astrological sense that men and women with strong natal Mars placements experience greater-than-average testosterone production, higher physical energy states, and can show more aggressive and competitive behavior.

When the natal Mars force enters a state of shock through any combination of transpersonal transits (from Uranus, Neptune or Pluto) testosterone levels may fluctuate wildly and influence the sex drive. Periods of accelerating sexual heat and arousal can often erupt and unexpectedly dissipate into an absence of libido, as if the Martial force went underground or was suspended. As the Mars force oscillates, so do the overall drive, desires and passions connected with it.

Part Two:
Jupiter, Saturn, Chiron, Uranus, Neptune and Pluto

Jupiter

Adventurous sex expands consciousness beyond belief. This can occur when courting strangers in unfamiliar situations or in foreign cultures. When there's a strong attraction to someone from a different ethnic, ideological, cultural and/or racial background, Jupiter may be involved. Sometimes, this exotic eroticism can turn into a *consciousness-expansion experiment* disguised as a relationship. Though Jupiter sex can expand awareness, it does not necessarily assure genuine awareness of the other.

It can be easy to overlook genuine differences—such as conflicts of values or mindsets—that can undermine compatibility. Imagine two people falling in love who do not speak the same language, literally or figuratively; it happens all the time. Lovers with profound ideological differences may also try to convert the other to their own cultural or moral values in an attempt to stay together. This could be symbolized by natal Jupiter conjunct Descendant or in the 7th or 8th House, Venus in Sagittarius or the 9th House, Gemini Rising, as well as transits and aspects with Jupiter.

Reckless Sex

Sometimes when natal Jupiter is activated, a kind of freewheeling, reckless spirit can be unleashed. There may be an excitement for noncommittal sexual liaisons with the already married or the unavailable lover, sex with the emotionally immature, or sex with someone you don't really care about. These sexual experiences can expand consciousness *via negativa* when lovers seek out ethically questionable experiences to test their conscience. As consciousness expands through these ethical tests, we may recognize what we actually care about—and don't care about—at all. As sex becomes more ethical, the beloved ceases to exist as an objectified extension of oneself. In deeper conscientious sex, the beloved can be seen in his, or her, own light, in what Martin Buber refers to as *the awareness of Thou.* Sex with conscience.

Saturn

Saturn symbolizes the psychological grip for asserting enough effort, structure and pressure to hold things together in a world that seems committed to falling apart. When Saturn becomes a strong force in any sexual relationship, certain kinds of holding patterns can appear. When someone holds you to your word, that is a holding pattern. When your lover holds you to a duty or to upholding a responsibility, that is a holding pattern. When someone else's natal Saturn closely aspects your natal Sun, Moon, Mars or Venus, their Saturn holding patterns put the pressure on you to be more accountable in those areas. If they are holding you to manage your life where it is falling apart, you may not like it but you will feel the pressure of being held to it anyway. You may even like it. A lot.

The Container and the Contained

Saturn's holding patterns can also be felt as a sensation of being contained by your lover or being the one containing the other. This dynamic of *the contained and the container* is a common structure in many relationships. Certain Saturn aspects (squares, oppositions, conjunctions) between lovers can symbolize an ongoing expression of latent parent/child dynamics. These can play out through an exposure of immature, infantile need-structures and latent paternal and maternal instincts. One lover plays out the Child, and the other, the Adult or parent role. It could be Mother or Father, Priest or Policeman, whatever floats the Saturn boat. Though not to be confused with literal incest, these parent/child dynamics can sometimes expose, address and heal early childhood abuse, sexual and otherwise.

Saturn sex tests the integrity and staying power of any relationship where the lovers consistently take on the same role as parent or child. If and when they discover that it's more responsibility or restriction than either care for, the current relationship structure can become brittle and fracture, begging for change. If the stronger Saturn person keeps making the weaker Saturn one feel inadequate, resentment and contempt can corrode the relationship and even end it. In this way, Saturnine holding patterns can also act out as boundary disputes or in the power sex playground of sadomasochism rituals.

Master/Slave Games

With mutual consent, unconscious power-tripping can be made conscious and transformed into power sex, where lovers take on submissive and dominant roles. This occurs through playful dramatization of scenarios involving various postures of trusting dominance and willing submission. Traditional S/M sex culture incorporates whips, chains, leather and other sex toys for ritualized power sex games. Power sex doesn't exist without a dominatrix or master and a slave or sub (submissive). The slave and dominatrix, or master, must first agree on the game plans. Leather harnesses, chains and handcuffs may be introduced by the master or dominatrix to increase the slave's pleasure, pressure, intensified sensation, and pain inside a climate of mutual trust. To respect the pain threshold, a "safe word" is agreed upon to stop all activity when spoken.

Though traditional S/M tribal sex culture relies on a vast array of ritual paraphernalia, none of it is necessary for power sex between consenting adults. The key element remains trust between lovers, and a ritual structure allowing for open expression of needs, fantasies and desires. Some have a greater need to be acted on by the saturnine holding pattern of another; others may need to be the ones holding that power to act on the other. As this sexual give-and-take process is openly explored, trust is built alongside greater sexual self-knowledge and a keener understanding of everyone's needs.

Role Reversals

In any given relationship where dominant-submissive patterns prevail, it's only a matter of time before roles get fixed and tensions start mounting. If either lover over-identifies with, and ends up fixating on one side of the dominant/submissive polarity, imbalance ensues. The passively identified grow more demure and meek as the dominant becomes more aggressive and cruel. Sooner or later these pressures can force confrontations, outbursts and explosions. Violence can erupt. When this happens, the lovers may be ready for role-reversal games.

Role reversals can balance lopsided relationship dynamics with the empathy to see through the other's eyes. If lovers cannot agree to walk in each other's shoes once in a while, their relationship dynamic can remain rigid and unstable. If mundane role reversals don't work, they may try the bedroom where the old master becomes the new slave and the old slave, the new master. Excitement for role reversals can sometimes restore relationship equilibrium.

The Arrangements

More volatile relationships may require a shared structure or routine to stabilize, such as working out together at the gym or taking long walks or playing many sets of tennis. When lovers share strong Saturn aspects, their sexual desires can also diminish over the years. If they still want to remain together, they might agree on a new relationship structure, a kind of *arrangement,* to stay together as companions or, perhaps, as creative collaborators. This shift requires a certain maturity to get beyond obsolete romantic ideals of love to meet newly emerging needs that can actually deepen the love and commitment between them.

Chiron

Transpersonal sex shocks the ego past itself into new ways of responding to energies greater than itself. Chirotic (rhymes with erotic) sex arouses the sleeping serpent of kundalini, enlivening the spinal cord with undulating, pulsating electrical charge. When lovers are connected chirotically by transit and/or synastry aspects, they may experience a kind of *tantric initiation of the third point.* When sexual energy between lovers escalates beyond what either lover can contain, that energy can either disperse or it can be redirected to a third point of awareness beyond both of them. This could be a shared goal they wish to energize into manifestation. It could be a more organic redirection of electrical charge down to the planet itself, stabilizing their bond at higher levels of sacred planetary love. (Refer to "Part Three: A Planetary Ménage a Trois".)

Uranus

Electric sex hums and pulses throughout the subtle medium of our Central Nervous System (CNS), igniting the lovers' energetic bodies (aura & chakras) as well as their physicality. Psychic, or electric, sex occurs through physical sex but can also happen without physical contact. When the CNS is energetically lit, sensuality transmutes into the supersensual brain pleasure of neurological orgasm.

As the CNS becomes self-aware, lovers respond to the warm, glowing rushes of neuroelectric signals racing within, around and between them. On more social levels, Uranus can represent group sex, orgies, threesomes, foursomes and then some. Uranian sex often involves heightened experimentation and a discovery of novel experiences within gender fluid intimacy.

Electromagnetic Sex

Electromagnetic sex can erupt unexpectedly in spontaneous and wildly uninhibited physical sex where signals traverse between brain and body at light speed. Amplification of electromagnetism in the body can activate telepathy, clairvoyance and a heightened awareness of synchronicity. This energy races through the muscles giving the Central Nervous System greater freedom of expression through spontaneous Mudras, or hand gestures.

When lovers can no longer sustain these higher levels of electromagnetic intimacy, they may start acting out their own egotistical habits of self-preoccupation until the charge fades away. In this way the ego acts as a kind of buffer for minimizing an experience too intense or volatile to contain. *How much rapture and brain pleasure can be allowed?* When the capacity for ecstasy becomes overwhelmed, to calm down it may be necessary to fixate on something as banal and mundane as personal problems.

Sex Magick

When higher levels of electromagnetic sex are desired with less ego, lovers may be ready to explore the esoteric methods of sex magick. Occult lodges such as the Hermetic Order of the Golden Dawn, the Ordo Templi Orientis (O.T.O.), and their numerous offshoots practice various ritual technologies for raising kundalini through sex magick practices. Long-term effects of sex magick can result in a radical transformation of the CNS. With some sex magick adepts, this change can be so remarkable that, when compared to the majority of humans, they can seem almost like alien space beings. There's probably good reason why these magickal ritual disciplines remain esoteric and hidden from mainstream view. *Sex magick isn't for everybody.*

Neptune

Transpersonal Neptune symbolizes the dreambody within us that awakens in our nocturnal dreams. It also refers to what aboriginal people know as *the dreamtime*. The elusive archetype of Neptune beckons us from realms so far beyond reason, so utterly alien and extraterrestrial to rationality, that the imagination must stretch itself simply to catch fleeting glimpses. Neptune governs out-of-body experiences, astral travel, and sexual experiences that induce various trances of hypnagogic visions. After powerful orgasms, the soul can drift out of body through ineffable experiences that escape words and then, back to the body as if returning from another world—the otherworldly, post-orgasm sex of Neptune.

Sex with Archetypes

Neptune also symbolizes the archetype of the Dream Lover, sometimes called the Animus and the Anima, that can take on the appearance in the dream of someone we know in waking life.

Visitations from archetypal presences disguised as people we know can arouse us sexually in dreams and leave us aroused after waking. These Neptune sex dreams may arrive when imagination needs a boost or when there's a transpersonal need for experiencing realities greater and more fantastical than the banality of mundane existence.

Nonstop Catastrophic Romances

Neptune transits to Venus, the Moon, Mercury, or through the 5th or 7th Houses, can coincide with wild, high-flying romances that yield no hope for a lasting relationship in the real world. When expectations during these courtships are not reality-based, the lovers embark on a nonstop catastrophic romance. They are catastrophic to the ego, yet strangely triumphant to the soul, bringing the timeless experience of infinite consciousness into the finite ego.

These fatal attractions can spiral into whirlpools of intoxicating delirium dispersing personal energy and distracting focus away from daily responsibilities. Lovers can become as zombies, psychic vampires draining each other or wrecking reputations, homes and families in the name of their "great love." Neptune can be very severe and slippery that way, mixing our highest hopes and ideals with our most devastating disillusionments and heartbreaks. When the fantasy of sex overwhelms the senses, awareness of another becomes obscured and diminished.

Anima/Animus

Neptune transits to natal Venus, Moon or Mercury can coincide with love affairs that begin and maintain themselves by a profound infatuation triggering the psychic projections of what psychologist Carl Jung calls "Anima/Animus transference." The Anima represents the image of the Ideal Feminine in the heterosexual man, often modeled after his mother, and can form the basis for his sexual fantasies of the Ideal Woman—the Goddess, the Woman of His Dreams. The Animus represents the image of the Ideal

Masculine in the heterosexual woman, often modeled after her father, and can form the basis for her sexual fantasies of the Dream Lover.

The psychic image of the Anima ignites and gets projected outwardly when a man encounters an actual woman whose appearance somehow matches the inner Anima. After this projection, the man becomes convinced he has met "the woman of his dreams" or "the One" whether or not the actual woman agrees or even cares for him. He may have actually met the woman of his nightmares and not know it until his projections collapse after she fails to live up to his unrealistic expectations. If the woman is made to feel inadequate, she can become resentful and make life difficult for him for as long as he continues with the Anima projections.

Similar scenarios can play out for the woman and her projections of the Animus archetype onto a man who matches her inner image. The overall purpose of these psychic projections of the Anima and Animus may be to expose the force and presence of the soul as it is thrown away onto the other. In the wake of these projections, the lover can feel abandoned and project their feelings of abandonments onto their lover. Closer to the truth may be how each lover has abandoned themselves through these projections while outwardly projecting *abandonment blame.*

Psychic projections of soul substance onto another requires time to heal, not just over the breakup of a relationship, but to restore the inner lives of the lovers. This healing period can be characterized as a personal process of *soul-retrieval,* of getting your soul back, through whatever experiences restore the sense of personhood and well-being.

Sometimes, when this Anima and Animus idea is first discovered, there can be an erroneous assumption that these archetypes belong to us. These archetypes don't belong to anyone, and may be best respected as *the* Anima and *the* Animus, rather than *my* Anima or *her* Animus. Much of sexual attraction begins in the brain, in the psyche. In the world of Neptune, this means the realm of dreams, fantasy and imagination.

Experiential Astrology

(Though these Anima/Animus examples are presented within the context of the Hetero tribe, variations on this contrasexual theme can apply to all sexual persuasions and realities.)

The Auric Merging of Sex Without Sex

Lovers under the influence of Neptune's dreaming power can be enchanted by merely holding hands or getting lost in each other's luminous eyes. Dreambody sex happens through shared auric merging that temporarily dissolves personal boundaries within spiritual communion. These potent mergings can expose lovers to indelible impressions of all-encompassing unity, not just between them, but with all of life.

This can also happen under the influence of psychoactive agents or in the wake of traumatic experiences shared by lovers undergoing Neptune transits to Venus, the Moon, or Mercury. These psychic links shared between lovers persist beyond time and space. Each can feel, see and sense the other over great distances, or hear each other's thoughts (telepathy, clairaudience), or appear in each other's dreams at night.

Virtual Sex

Futuristic forms of manufactured illusory Neptunian sex are fast becoming popular as pornography industries get in bed with sophisticated virtual reality (VR) immersion software. Consumers are promised virtual sex "beyond their wildest dreams" and many will choose these corporate-simulations over the real thing. Milder versions of virtual sex are found in online community bulletin boards, CD-ROM interactive sex games, and chatroom sex fantasy role-playing sites where sex begins and ends in the imagination and the digitization of the sexual response.

Pluto

At the deepest level of sexual reality, Pluto symbolizes the invisible processes of conception and gestation and the passage from the womb through the birth canal. Plutonic procreational sex can erupt whenever the genetic conduits, the DNA matrix within each lover, are activated with overwhelming surges to bring a child into this world. Oftentimes, this genetic force can dominate any moral or intellectual argument with it. Lovers may come together for reasons of procreation without knowing it until pregnancy occurs, transforming their reasons for staying together or parting ways. DNA is carried by the powerful plutonic agenda of living forever or die trying.

The womb and reproductive system are a powerful source and engine of creation, symbolizing Pluto's transformative powers that also find expression beyond childbirth. Cultural and familial pressures to procreate can confuse some women who may not be meant to bear children, whose wombs are meant to serve another purpose of creation. Women artists who also desire children stand at the crossroads between sacrificing their lives to Motherhood or to Art. The sad truth is not every woman can do both and do both well. Though some can, many who attempt both in the same time period end up doing one or both poorly or are forced into the heartbreak of having to give up Art or Motherhood.

Beyond Procreation

Certain kinds of plutonic sexual energies do not produce offspring but somehow advance the evolutionary imperatives of DNA in other ways. What characterizes any evolutionary imperative of DNA? The discovery of novel models of intimacy and new ways of being human—*Homo Novus, mutation of the new human.*

Evolutionary shocks can occur during Pluto transits to Mars, Venus and the Moon, super-charging visceral and romantic sexual response far beyond socially-accepted norms. Sometimes the sheer power of these plutonic forces can feel like they're so much bigger than the physical body; they can feel impossible to contain. These experiences can be confusing as to their purpose. *What's going on? Why is this happening? Where do I put all this energy?*

Some Pluto transits—*conjunctions and oppositions to the Moon, Venus, Mars and Sun*—can be synchronized with powerfully transformative psychosexual encounters that have little or nothing to do with falling in love, having a "relationship," getting married, making babies, domesticating or buying furniture. These plutonic encounters may not fit into any existing categories like "hot sex," "casual sex," "one-night stands," or "affairs."

Sometimes these plutonic energies can be transformed through art, or sublimated and circulated through the larger body of transpersonal causes. But if none of these outlets or options fit, then what? Something like this happened to me in the summer of 1988 that inspired the writing of my book, *The Akashic Record Player*. This transformative plutonic event occurred spontaneously with a total stranger and it changed my life. Read on...

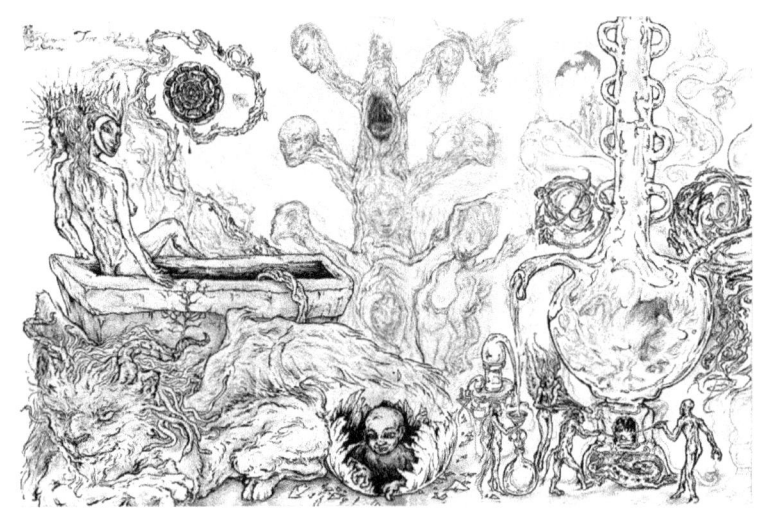

Part Three:
A Planetary Ménage à Trois
Wherein the Author Submits to the Earth

Experiential Astrology

I have come to understand and know the Earth as a highly intelligent and compassionate entity incarnating as this planet. This vision was born from an uncommon experience that happened to me and a woman I met near Boulder, Colorado on the eve of Summer Solstice, 1988. I had never seen her before this encounter and have not seen or heard from her since, nor have I wanted to. In retrospect, our meeting seemed as if arranged by the planetary entity for a mysterious (to us) ritual feeding of the Earth.

I was walking on a path in the foothills of the Rockies when I noticed a woman walking towards me. When we were about five feet from each other, we stopped and stood there, eyes wide open, no words. A calm, quiet, magnetic waveform started pulsating between us. We slowly sat down at the same time, facing each other. Still no words, eyes wide open. The sun had started to set.

Sitting across from each other, our faces faintly trembled with questions: *Who are you? What is this? Where is this going?* Still, no spoken words. I thought of introducing myself, but all I could do was smile, thinking, "I am not my name." I didn't even know who I was in this moment. She smiled back at me, as if thinking the same thing. The electromagnetism pulsating between us became stronger, denser, and I felt or heard a barely discernible buzzing hum. I felt sexually aroused and felt that she was aroused too, but there was something too new, too different about this. All I could do was just be still and maintain eye contact with her.

The energy moving between us was now felt like it was circulating throughout my entire body. She nodded as if noticing this. Whatever force was moving through me was becoming stronger and creating a gentle pressure inside me. As this pressure increased, I started breathing faster; my pulse started racing. With every inhale, I remember feeling the energy of the earth enter me, and with every exhale, this earth energy began circulating throughout my body. I continued this breathing cycle—*inhaling earth energy, exhaling to circulate*—while looking into her eyes. My pulse slowed down. I felt very alert, but also very calm.

Eye contact now became more difficult as her face started going in and out of focus before disappearing altogether. What I was looking at, seeing really, was not her face, but a sphere of light (she later disclosed that she saw the same sphere of light after my face disappeared). This frightened me for a moment, and then her face suddenly reappeared. I returned to my breathing. Deeper breaths, slowing the pulse.

This earth-connected breathing cycle stabilized my energy field into the hyper-alert state of deep calm I felt before. That's when she reached out to me, palms out, placing both of her hands on my chest. I felt a cool rush of bluish force entering my heart and mixing with the earth energy circulating throughout my body. After an eternal moment, she spoke. Three words: *Feed the earth.*

Intuitively, it became clear that all the earth energy circulating throughout my body was not meant entirely for me; *it was not even my energy.* On each inhale, I kept circulating the energy, but now, on each exhale, I directed this energy down into the planet. My body felt like it was becoming a kind of conduit mixing and circulating energy for feeding the planet. Questions arose in me. What was really happening? What was her role here? She removed her hands from my chest and crossed them over her heart while rocking gently, eyes closed. I continued feeding the earth while watching her slow, rapturous rocking.

The sun had set some time ago; it was dark and impossible to tell how long we were there. The ritual felt like it was over or maybe my body was just spent by all that high energy. We stood up and walked down the path in the direction she came from. That's when we both started talking, asking questions. *What was that? Who are you? Where is this going? Does this mean we're lovers? Did we know each other in a past life? Should we flee from each other or get married?*

Every answer we came up with either felt fake or just exploded or fell apart. We laughed. We laughed a lot. Laughing never felt so good. We knew something miraculous had happened, and that we were part of it, but we had no words or explanations for what felt deeply profound, but also totally absurd. We laughed some more and then we arrived at her car. Without a word, she drove me to the area where my car was parked. No goodbyes, no exchange of phone numbers. We hugged for what felt like an hour but was probably only a minute. And then I left. We never knew each other's names nor did we share any personal history. The experience changed my life.

Postscript

Unbeknownst to me at the time this event happened, the transit of Pluto was passing through the State of the Soul in my chart while opposing my 6th house Taurus Jupiter and squaring my Nodal Axis, forming a kind of virtual grand fixed cross. To read more on this "Earth Surrender Rite", refer to my book *The Akashic Record Player: A Non-Stop Geomantic Conspiracy* (1988, Falcon Press).

AFTERWORD

The experiential bias behind writing this book mirrors the bias guiding my life for as long as I can remember. I hope what readers take away from reading this book is the idea that your actual life matters—*not the life you think you should or could've had, if only things were different.* I'm talking about the life you're actually living, whether you currently like that life or not, or whether you are even aware of the life you are *actually living.*

Being unaware of the life you are actually living may be more common than you think. A pervasive collective influence of *cultural trance* keeps many of us asleep to our actual lives. This culturally-induced amnesia makes it easy to forgot our true selves and take on false identities and values manufactured by the public education systems, the advertising and entertainment industries, churches and religions, and all the books and teachers that taught us what to think but never showed us *how to think.*

The experiential bias of this book does not dismiss theories, speculations or assumptions unless they fail to respect the existing conditions of things; *respect existence or expect resistance.* At best, astrology can open the doors of perception and offer new ways of seeing. As Carl Jung discovered, it can act as an effective diagnostic tool in psychotherapy, but alas, astrology makes for a crappy treatment plan. There's only so much that *talk therapy* can do to alleviate the grip of unconscious complexes.

It may not be enough to merely understand or comprehend your horoscope—or any dimension of yourself—if you cannot experience it for yourself beyond the observer position. Experiential Astrology (XA) can be a means to access and engage the very forces governing our existence for those with the courage and audacity to embrace and embody the energies symbolized by the planets. Who has the nerve to live a magical life?

If our life lacks a constant magic, it is because we choose to observe our acts and lose ourselves in consideration of their imagined form instead of being impelled by their force. No matter how loudly we

clamor for magic in our lives, we are really afraid of pursuing an existence entirely under its influence and sign.
— Antonin Artaud

Every bias has its *anti-bias*. When you stand firmly enough behind one view then, by default, you may also stand against its opposite. The opposite of an experiential bias might be any *theoretical bias or rhetorical bias* that forgoes the authenticity of personal experience by adhering instead to untested generalizations, rhetoric and theories.

An astrological example of an anti-experiential bias can be found in the countless astrology newsletters, columns, blogs and books that interpret current transits for everyone with broad strokes of impersonal generalizations. Here's an example: *"When Mars opposes Uranus, passions run hot, tempers flare, and impulses quicken."* Naive readers may assume that "passions will run hot, tempers flare, and impulses quicken" for everyone during this time period. *No, it won't apply to everybody.* When those reading these forecasts believe what they're told it's easy to see why astrology and astrologers are so often ridiculed.

What's missing from these generalized astrological forecasts is any indication of whether or not transiting Mars or Uranus is actually aspecting anything in one's personal horoscope. Those who study astrology and have a rudimentary understanding of their own horoscope may know what I mean.

If transiting Uranus is at 14 degrees Taurus and you know that your Moon is at 14 degrees Scorpio, you can understand how your inner, emotional life may undergo a temporary destabilizing period as a prelude to experiencing more freedom. Does Uranus cause these changes? No, it doesn't. The transit of Uranus measures *the timing of change, not its cause.* The true sources of change in our lives may be more complex than we think; they may be more complex than we *can* think.

Wiser astrology columns, such as Rob Brezsny's *Free Will Astrology*, forecast situations each week for all twelve Sun signs based on transits to the Rising Sign. In other words, the horoscope message for Scorpios is based on the positions of transiting planets in a Scorpio Rising chart; his column also works if you know your Rising sign. Since Rob is also a poet, his language is often infused with evocative imagery and quotations from literary figures, artists, scientists and mythology. Combining these factors, *Free Will Astrology* gets as close to an experiential bias that Sun sign astrology columns can get.

When any of the outer three planets—*Uranus, Neptune and Pluto*—pass from the end of one sign into the beginning of the next sign, it marks the end of an era and the start of another. World history has demonstrated how these outer planet transits have synchronized with larger impersonal collective shifts giving way to the emerging zeitgeists of social, economic and political change. Sometimes our personal lives become deeply impacted by these larger impersonal forces, weaving us into the greater fabric of history in the making. This can happen when these transpersonal transits directly aspect the personal forces symbolized in our horoscopes. These transits can also go by unnoticed, as if nothing is happening at all—one of many ways astrology can be mysterious; sometimes astrology works, and sometimes it doesn't.

Though this book was written during the Covid pandemic, another virus has surfaced that may be just as contagious and, in some ways, deadlier. I refer to the ubiquitous Fundamentalist Virus (FV) currently infecting the collective mindset through the superspreaders of religion, politics, science, school systems, government policies, and yes, even astrology. Symptoms of the FV appear daily as overly literalist thinking, manic scapegoating, dogmatic bigotry, ungrounded assumptions, and overwhelming groupthink. Add to this the tragic loss and death of the Imagination, the chief inlet of Soul in the hyper-digital era, and we have a real-world problem.

Though no time-tested vaccines have been approved to combat the FV, periodic booster shots of accelerated perception, creativity and empathy have proven effective during transits from Uranus, Neptune and Pluto as they aspect the personal forces (planets) of the Sun, Mercury, Mars, Jupiter, Venus, the Moon, and the Ascendant (in one's horoscope) by conjunction, square and/or opposition.

Though no cure or immunity can be absolute, alleviation of this dreary, dismal disease is now available to those who can still think for themselves, love with an open heart, and possess enough will to fight for what makes their life worth living. If you are still capable of having an actual experience—beyond the countless *simulations of experience* offered in today's digitized world—you are developing cultural immunity. Culture here refers to *the toxic culture* that diminishes the human capacity for experience and its incumbent atrophy of imagination, of discovering and creating images of your own.

Over my thirty-five years of astrological practice, it has become clear that my skill and talent for interpreting horoscopes have developed through two parallel orientations. The first orientation continues as an ongoing study of astrology as a language that helps me communicate my perceptions to others. This first orientation has filled my head with multitudes of ideas and insights about how astrology works, but not why it works; I don't know why astrology works and I don't need to know.

The second orientation persists in a capacity for freeing my mind of astrology—to think, intuit and articulate my everyday impressions independent of astrological symbols and references. For me, astrology has been most effective as a tool; when I'm done using the tool, it goes back into the toolbox. I'm not in love with astrology; *I'm in love with life.* Some astrologers may exclaim, "But astrology *is* life!" and to them, I say, "Well, maybe astrology is *your* life."

This freedom from over-identifying with any esoteric system is well-symbolized by my 9th house Uranus opposing 3rd house Mars and their participation in a T-Square with my 11th house Saturn/Neptune conjunction (and its release into the target zone of the Creative State of my 5th house). My joy experienced as an artist depends on an open, healthy relationship with uncertainty *as a creative state,* an outlook that alleviates the anxiety I see others suffering from. In my mind, anxiety can be managed by learning to permit more uncertainty. Since uncertainty remains a fact of everyday life, courting unknowns allows me to live my *actual* life.

Though the title of "astrologer" is no longer something I identify with, I don't mind others thinking of me in this way. I stopped identifying with any self-image during my early forties when the transit of Pluto conjunct my 12th house Sun and Ascendant while opposing natal 6th house Jupiter. Did Pluto stop me from having a self-image? Of course not; facing my ego-naïveté stopped me. Up until this transit, I had a grand old time identifying as "The Published Author", "The Theatre Director", "The Teacher", "The Professional Astrologer"; I was shamelessly full of myself. All these fancy-pants self-images exploded into smithereens during the timing of this Pluto transit which also heralded the sudden death of my very young daughter, Zoe, in September of 1992.

Pluto is said to govern all processes of death and rebirth, though not every Pluto transit synchronizes with personal catastrophe. Apparently, I was ripe for it. My experience of *ego-death* underwent many stages and emotions—*grief, rage, helplessness, despair, depression, bewilderment, disorientation, awakening*—before rebirth eventually blossomed through the medium of cinema. Redeemed by art, my first feature underground film, "The Oracle", was made six months after losing Zoe and I have continued making feature art films ever since. The transformation experienced during this Pluto transit was also no mere *change of state* but a powerful transformation of my very being (the Sun).

In closing this Afterword, I must express my deep gratitude for Sylvi, my partner in art and in life, for her undying devotion over the last twenty-six hundred years. Sylvi's music, her songs, and her voice bring my films to life—echoing the Music of the Spheres, when the planets hum their celestial harmonics while orbiting the Sun, an exquisite alchemy that has enlivened and defined our lives.

— Antero Alli, 12.21.2021

ABOUT THE AUTHOR

Antero Alli has written three astrology books: *Astrologik*; *Letters, Essays and Premonitions: An Astrological Journal*; and *Experiential Astrology: From the Map to the Territory*. His other books include *Angel Tech: A Modern Shaman's Guide to Reality Selection*; *The Eight-Circuit Brain: Navigational Strategies for the Energetic Body*; *Towards an Archeology of the Soul*; *The Akashic Record Player: A Non-Stop Geomantic Conspiracy*; and *State of Emergence: Experiments in Group Ritual Dynamics*. Over the past four decades he has also written, directed and produced fourteen feature art films as well as numerous experimental theatre works. Discover more about his products and services at: verticalpool.com

FROM ANTERO ALLI

ANGEL TECH
A Modern Shaman's Guide to Reality Selection

Angel Tech is a comprehensive compendium of insights and techniques for the direct application of Dr. Timothy Leary's Eight-Circuit Brain model for Intelligence Increase. What Dr. Leary posited as theory and Dr. Robert Anton Wilson brilliantly demonstrated in sociopolitical, mathematical and intellectual proofs, Antero Alli has extended into tangible tasks, exercises, rituals and meditations.

THE EIGHT-CIRCUIT BRAIN
Navigational Strategies for the Energetic Body

The Eight-Circuit Brain advances and expands the material presented in *Angel Tech,* a compendium of techniques and practical applications based on Dr. Timothy Leary's 8-Circuit Brain model. After more than twenty years of research and experimentation, Antero's earlier findings are significantly updated and enriched.

FROM ANTERO ALLI

A MODERN SHAMAN'S GUIDE TO A PREGNANT UNIVERSE
With Christopher S. Hyatt, Ph.D.

The Pregnant Universe is a Neural Cocktail party of a brain getting drunk on itself. It is the essence of slimy copulation between known and unknown forces. As the planet braces for a series of new contractions, bizarre and interesting forces are being born—brains with new centers, new chemicals, new visions—going far beyond the suited dinosaurs prattling their slogans.

REBELS & DEVILS
The Psychology of Liberation

Contributions by Antero Ali, Wm. S. Burroughs, Timothy Leary, Robert Anton Wilson, Aleister Crowley, A.O. Spare, Jack Parsons, Genesis P-Orridge, and many, many others.

"When he put the gun to my head at 16 I left home…" So begins this remarkable book which brings together some of the most talented, controversial and rebellious people *ever*. Not to be missed!

FROM ANTERO ALLI

PARATHEATRE
A Ritual Technology for Self-Initiation

Since 1977, Antero Alli has been developing a ritual technology for Self-Initiation—Paratheatre—combining techniques of theatre, dance and zazen to access and express the internal landscape. Paratheatre is highly transformative and has served as a critical source of inspiration for many of Antero's artistic endeavors, especially his films. (Two Audio CDs)

8-CIRCUITS OF CONSCIOUSNESS

In this video, Antero Alli discusses his research results and a wide variety of perceptions on Timothy Leary's 8-Circuit Brain model for Intelligence Increase. Antero introduces the origin of this system and how his interpretations differ from Dr. Leary's and Robert Anton Wilson's, along with his insights on the vertical connectivities between upper and lower circuits, the function and nature of shock, the first and second attentions and much, much more.

FROM ANTERO ALLI

TO DREAM OF FALLING UPWARDS

The elder Magus just passed away. Jack Mason, a promising young sex magickian cultivated to advance the lineage, loses it all when the elder Magus' biological son unexpectedly inherits everything with plans to commercialize and franchise the Temple. Jack plots deadly revenge and falls into a dizzying maze of encounters with underworld characters, desert brujas, and a twist of fate he never saw coming...or did he? (DVD)

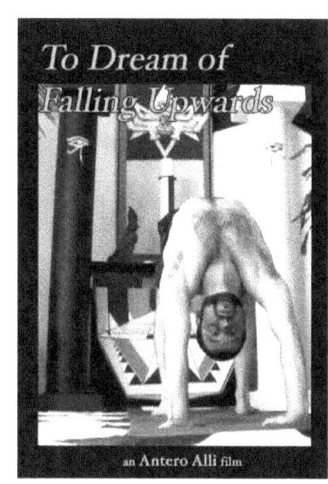

UNDER A SHIPWRECKED MOON

The power of a long-dead family secret is unleashed when the rituals of a self-made shamanic punk rocker catapult him into the spirit realm in search of his father, a ship's captain who drowned at sea. Meanwhile, back in the real world, he and his family gather around the bedside of his grandfather who has suddenly reappeared after a fifteen year absence. A surrealistic fable of love, giant hedgehogs, and the mystical depths of family bonds. (DVD)

THE *Original* FALCON PRESS

Invites You to Visit Our Website:
http://originalfalcon.com

At our website you can:

- Browse the online catalog of all of our great titles
- Find out what's available and what's out of stock
- Get special discounts
- Order our titles through our secure online server
- Find products not available anywhere else including:
    - One of a kind and limited availability products
    - Special packages
    - Special pricing
- Get free gifts
- Join our email list for advance notice of New Releases and Special Offers
- Find out about book signings and author events
- Send email to our authors
- Read excerpts of many of our titles
- Find links to our authors' websites
- Discover links to other weird and wonderful sites
- And much, much more

Get online today at http://originalfalcon.com

www.ingramcontent.com/pod-product-compliance
Lightning Source LLC
LaVergne TN
LVHW021701060526
838200LV00050B/2450